Commonly blamed as the man who started World War I, Kaiser Wilhelm II of Germany is often seen as a tough aggressor; a man, as Bismarck might have said, "of blood and iron". As leader of the world's strongest army, he wielded great power. When, at the beginning of this century, he built up an almost equally strong navy, it seemed as if nothing could stop Germany's advance.

But was he really the strong man of popular legend? Richard Garrett argues that, behind the stern appearance and the flamboyant moustache, Kaiser Bill was a failure. He believed that God had appointed him Emperor of Germany, and that God would tell him what do. His talent for making enemies was enormous. He had grown up as a spoilt child with a wide knowledge of many things and a deep understanding of almost nothing. As a diplomat he was liable to gross misjudgments; and yet his arrogant faith in himself never faltered.

This is the story of the effect of one man on thirty years of world history, culminating in a monstrous clash of arms and ending in the quietness of exile. Out of the story a picture of the real man emerges, and the events which led up to the disaster are put into their true perspective. Was it the Kaiser, more than anyone else, who unwittingly prepared the way for Hitler? This book may suggest an answer.

Kaiser Bill

Richard Garrett

More Wayland Kings and Queens

George III	Amanda Purves
Alfred the Great	Jennifer Westwood
Mary Queen of Scots	Alan Bold
Elizabeth I	Alan Kendall
James I	David Walter
Charles I	Hugh Purcell
Charles II	Michael Gibson
Louis XIV	Christopher Martin
Peter the Great	Michael Gibson
Catherine the Great	Miriam Kochan
Napoleon I	Stephen Pratt
Queen Victoria	Richard Garrett

Frontispiece Wilhelm II in the
uniform of a colonel of the British
Dragoons.

SBN 85340 436 4

Copyright © 1978 by Wayland (Publishers) Ltd
First published in 1978
by Wayland (Publishers) Ltd,
49 Lansdowne Place, Hove, East Sussex BN3 1HF

Printed in Great Britain by
Butler & Tanner Ltd, Frome and London

Contents

I The Child of Destiny

ON A JUNE EVENING IN 1858, a rocket streaked its sparkling path across the sky above London. On a hot summer's day in 1914, the first shell of World War I exploded on the soil of Europe. Between the two lay more than half a century, but in a way the inoffensive firework ignited a trail of events that ended in war.

The firework display was one of the diversions arranged to celebrate the wedding of Victoria, Princess Royal, eldest child of Queen Victoria and Prince Albert, to Frederick William ("Fritz"), heir apparent to the Prussian throne. The young couple had become engaged at Balmoral a year previously. Now, on 25th June, 1858, they were married in St James's Chapel. The bride was barely eighteen years old, the bridegroom was twenty-seven. But there was more to the union than the love of a prince and a princess. As the Prince Consort saw it, the occasion marked the betrothal of Britain to Prussia.

Germany at that time was a collection of miscellaneous states. Some of them were reasonably large, others minute. Industrially they were backward; socially, feudal; and (with the exception of Prussia) they had small sense of national pride.

1848 had been a year of revolution in Europe—a year when the old autocracies were questioned, and the breeze of a new and more liberal order blew across the Continent. Louis-Philippe of France abdicated; there were riots in Venice, Vienna and Berlin. On 4th March, Frederick William IV agreed to merge Prussia with the rest of Germany, hoping to create a new kingdom. Two months later, a national assembly met at Frankfurt.

> "I clasped her in my arms and blessed her, and knew not what to say. I kissed good Fritz and pressed his hand again and again. He was unable to speak and the tears were in his eyes."
> *Queen Victoria, on the marriage of her daughter, Victoria, the Princess Royal, to Prince Frederick William of Prussia.*

Opposite An engagement picture of Wilhelm II's parents, Prince Frederick William of Prussia and the Princess Royal of Britain.

> **"I will repeat that a great liberal generous policy is the prerequisite of an alliance with England."** *The Prince Consort to Kaiser Wilhelm I.*

The men who met that day in the city's Paulskirche were far from representative. All of them came from the intellectual and professional classes and from the ranks of officialdom. Where were the big businessmen? The wage-earners? They were either at home, or else in their offices and factories; and yet, without their support, no unity was possible. It was not until 1866, eighteen years later, that there was the remotest chance that a man might be able to vote for somebody who actually understood his problems!

Prince Albert (a German by birth) continued to hope that this chaotic collection of states might yet become welded into a whole. He was determined that, when it occurred, unity would be on constitutional and liberal lines. He thought that his daughter Victoria's marriage would help his plans.

Below The wedding of Kaiser Bill's parents.

Queen Victoria supported her husband. The Prime Minister, Lord Palmerston, was less enthusiastic. But Palmerston took little more than a passing interest in German affairs. If this was what his royal employers wished, he did not intend to raise any objections to the match. Indeed, such difficulties as were created came from the Queen.

Her Majesty was told that it was customary for Prussian princes to be married in Berlin and the present match could not be regarded as an exception. When this information reached Queen Victoria, she dipped her ever-industrious pen into the nearest inkwell, and quickly wrote a note to the Prussian Ambassador.

The idea was not to be considered. His Excellency, she wrote, should "not *entertain* the *possibility* of such a question.... The Queen *never* could consent to it, both for public and private reasons, and the assumption of its being *too much* for a Royal Prince of Prussia to *come* over to marry the *Princess Royal of Great Britain* in England is too absurd to say the least.... Whatever may be the usual practice of Prussian princes, it is not *every* day that one marries the eldest daughter of the Queen of England. The question must therefore be considered as settled and closed."

They were a strangely-matched couple, this precocious girl and this quiet, almost humble, young man. The Prince Consort, who had nine children, believed that all but one were afraid of him. The exception was Victoria. She was unusually intelligent and she had a very strong will. The other royal children were often in trouble. Victoria could do no wrong.

As she grew up, she inherited a liberal outlook from her father; a love of England and its traditions from her mother; and her strength of character from both of them. The one thing she lacked was wisdom. She was unlikely to adapt herself to the ways of her new country.

It happened that at this particular moment in history the Princess's adopted land needed a lot of understanding—far more than she was prepared to give it. In the same year as the marriage, Frederick William IV of

"Unlike many German princesses married to foreigners, the home of her birth stood first with her to the end. Even one like myself, purely German and Prussian in thought and feeling, can understand and even honour such faithfulness: but it did lead to difficulties such as should be avoided between mother and son." *Kaiser Wilhelm II, on his mother.*

Above Otto von Bismarck, the powerful Prime Minister of Prussia. Later he was Chancellor of Germany under three sovereigns for thirty years.

"Take care of that man; he means what he says." *Disraeli, on Bismarck.*

Prussia was finally declared insane. He had been dithering on the edge of lunacy for some time. Now he was compelled to hand over power to his brother Wilhelm, Fritz's father. Three years later, in 1861, Frederick William died and Wilhelm succeeded him.

Basically, Wilhelm I was a simple soldier. He loved military parades and bands, and the old class structure—in which an officer corps of nobles (the Junkers) ruled a race of peasant soldiers.

Without a doubt Wilhelm had hankerings after glory. Unlike his ancestor Frederick the Great, however, he had not the qualities to achieve it. Somebody else was needed to supply the ideas and put them into action. As it happened, fate had just such a person in mind—Otto von Bismarck.

Everything about Bismarck was big, from the man himself to his country house, which seemed to be equipped with outsize furniture. He kept big dogs, used enormous pencils, had a personality almost as large as Prussia, and enjoyed immense visions of his country's future power.

In 1862 Wilhelm made Bismarck Prime Minister of Prussia. In 1871, after the German states had joined together, he was made a prince and became Imperial Chancellor.

According to Bismarck, no man should die until he had smoked one hundred thousand cigars and consumed five thousand bottles of champagne. It was a task to which he applied himself with enthusiasm! During these moments of relaxation, he was given to considering outstanding problems. The greatest of them seemed to be his sovereign's daughter-in-law. With her liberal views and her love of England, she represented everything the Chancellor detested.

Three years before the coming to power of this towering character, fate had slipped another actor on the stage. The year was 1859, and the newcomer was the young couple's first child, Wilhelm. Unfortunately what should have been a glorious moment in Prussian history was marred by an accident of birth. As he was

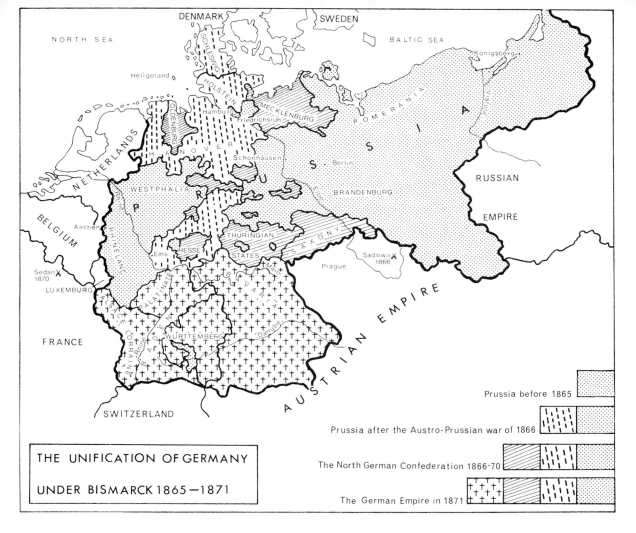

THE UNIFICATION OF GERMANY

UNDER BISMARCK 1865—1871

Prussia before 1865

Prussia after the Austro-Prussian war of 1866

The North German Confederation 1866-70

The German Empire in 1871

emerging from his mother's womb, one of the future ruler's arms became detached from its socket. As a result, it was shorter than the other—and virtually useless.

Before long, a war was raging between the forceful Princess and the no less assertive Chancellor. The point at issue was the development of a partially-infirm small boy. As for poor Fritz, with his thick beard and his blue, transparently honest eyes, he could only play the part of an unhappy spectator. He was like a man caught in a thunderstorm.

Above Young Wilhelm painfully learned to ride.

2 Growing-up

PRINCESS VICTORIA (or Crown Princess Frederick, as she was now called) did not like Berlin. She found the city narrow and provincial—quite the opposite of London. As for her husband's family, one suspects that they bored her with their nationalistic enthusiasm, and their inability to discuss anything other than the army, food and court politics. The disappointment of her son's deformity now added to her homesickness and general unhappiness.

Her husband was a mild-mannered man, already succumbing to her iron will. He had even taken on a British army officer, Lt Col Summerfield, as his private secretary. In later years, Summerfield was to observe that it was "absolutely inconceivable that Frederick should ever, no matter what the circumstances, assert his own will in opposition to his wife's. You have only to look at what she's made of him. But for her, he'd be the average man, very arrogant, good-tempered, of mediocre gifts and with a great deal of common sense. But *now*, he's not a man at all . . . he's a mere cipher."

Left to his own devices, the Crown Prince would doubtless have made allowances for his son's handicap, but his wife took a less gentle view. The boy should be subjected to the same upbringing as any other child. She was not content to ignore his small deformity: she seemed to regard it as a challenge. Indeed, she went to such lengths to inflict a spartan regime upon him, that it is hardly surprising young Wilhelm grew up in the belief that she hated him.

Victoria would have heatedly denied this. As she once wrote: "Willy is a dear, interesting charming boy—

> **"To me it seems that an education from which all joy is excluded is psychologically false."** *Wilhelm, on his upbringing.*

> **"He does not possess exactly brilliant abilities nor any other strength of character or talent.... I watch over him myself and every smallest detail of his education.... He possesses a strong constitution and would be a handsome lad if it were not for this unfortunate left arm which becomes more and more noticeable."** *Wilhelm's mother, about Wilhelm.*

clever, amusing, engaging—it is impossible not to spoil him a little!" Perhaps unknowingly, he inherited his mother's passion for most things English. Rudyard Kipling's *If* was said to be his favourite poem, and he once sent the author a telegram that could reasonably be described as "fan mail". He also enjoyed the works of Dickens, Scott, Kenneth Grahame, Bernard Shaw and P G Wodehouse. And he shared the English belief that fresh air was a preventative, if not actually a cure, for pretty well everything from attacks of depression to tuberculosis.

Strangely enough, the child's first memory was of a visit to his grandparents' home at Osborne on the Isle

Below The adult Wilhelm shooting from a butt on the Yorkshire moors. His host, the Earl of Lonsdale, made it impossible for him to miss and he bagged sixty brace of grouse in one day.

of Wight. He cannot have been more than two at the time, but he was able to recall how the Prince Consort had taken "a great deal of notice of his eldest little grandson, and used to dandle me in a table napkin". He had an even more vivid impression when he went to England at the age of four for the wedding of his uncle the Prince of Wales to the beautiful Princess Alexandra of Schleswig-Holstein-Sonderburg-Glucksburg, daughter of the King of Denmark. He liked the music of the Horse Guards, and professed to have been particularly fond of Mendelssohn's Wedding March from *A Midsummer Night's Dream*.

When Wilhelm visited Britain, he often proved to be a tiresome guest, even as a grown-up. His uncle, King Edward VII, remarked, "Willy is a bully and like most bullies, when tackled, is a coward." Another time, after a visit to Sandringham that severely taxed Edward's patience, the British King was heard to mutter, "Thank God he's gone." Wilhelm's eagerness to criticize affected everything from the hospitality he received to the rules of the Royal Yacht Squadron at Cowes. When out on a day's shooting, he was sensitive to the fact that his disability made him a poor marksman. Allowances had to be made by providing so much game that it was almost impossible for him to miss. Once, when staying with the Earl of Lonsdale, he returned from an outing with a bag of sixty-seven rabbits. The score was less impressive, when one realizes that six under-keepers concealed in the woods had released literally hundreds of the wretched animals. But Wilhelm was pleased. Afterwards, he presented his considerate host with a large marble bust of himself.

The birth of Wilhelm was followed in 1860 by the arrival of a sister, Charlotte. Thereafter, punctual almost to the day, the Crown Princess produced a child at two-yearly intervals until 1872, when Margaret was born. The final score was eight. Prince Henry (born in 1862) later distinguished himself in naval and motoring circles—a race and a Vauxhall car were named after him. Princess Sophia (born 1870) eventually married

"In the twinkle of an eye, the highest may find themselves at the feet of the poorest and lowest." *Queen Victoria uttering a warning about young Wilhelm's excessive pride.*

King Constantine I of Greece. Otherwise, the accomplishments and marriages of the young Hohenzollerns were undistinguished.

Victoria, as she herself admitted, was not a very satisfactory mother. Until young Sigismund died at the age of two in 1866, she tended to neglect her children. After that tragedy, she tried to make good this omission by an attention to Wilhelm's upbringing that was little short of stifling. The other were, perhaps, more fortunate; but they were not heirs to an emerging empire, nor did they suffer from physical handicaps. Consequently they were allowed to develop as nature, and not necessarily as Victoria, intended.

When Wilhelm was five years old, a tutor was appointed. His name was Dr George Hinzpeter. Hinzpeter was thirty-nine, the son of a philosophy professor and experienced in tutoring the sons of the nobility. Wilhelm remembered him as a "dry, pedantic [bookish] man, with his gaunt meagre figure, and parchment face". Hinzpeter was told to drive his pupil hard, and he seems to have accepted the instructions with relish. Lessons began at six a.m. in summer (seven o'clock in winter) and went on for twelve hours a day—with two breaks for food and exercise. If Wilhelm thought the word "exercise" meant pleasant games in the palace gardens, he was in for a rude shock. The task of attending to his physical development was entrusted to an infantry officer who was also told to spare the boy no extremes of discomfort.

The worst part was the riding instruction. It was, according to Hinzpeter, "at first actually dangerous and forced upon him with stern discipline, despite his tearful resistance.... When the Prince was eight and a half years old, a lackey still had to lead his pony by the rein, because his balance was so bad that his unsteadiness caused unbearable anxiety to himself and others. So long as this lasted, he could not learn to ride: it had to be overcome, no matter at what cost.... The tutor, using a moral authority over his pupil that by now had become absolute, set the weeping Prince on his horse, without stirrups and compelled him to go through the various paces. He fell off continually: every time, despite his prayers and tears, he was lifted up and set upon its back again. After weeks of torture, the difficult task was accomplished: he had got his balance."

And, despite his arm, he also became a better shot, proficient at sailing and rowing, and a very tolerable swimmer. As for his long lessons with Hinzpeter, he showed a creditable ability to absorb facts. He was less talented at drawing conclusions from them.

Such an upbringing was bound to produce a reaction in Wilhelm. Either he would become submissive like his father—or else he would become defiant. He became the latter. People around him noticed a growing arrogance. During a visit to his grandmother at Osborne, for example, she instructed him to bow to a distinguished visitor. Wilhelm refused. But such conduct was not tolerated by Queen Victoria. As Lytton Strachey wrote in his biography of Her Majesty: "The order was sternly repeated, and the naughty boy, noticing that his kind grandmama had suddenly turned into a most terrifying lady, submitted his will to hers, and bowed very low indeed."

During these difficult years, there was only one man for whom the boy felt complete affection—his grandfather, Wilhelm I. The old man and his small grandson would stand at a window of the palace and enjoy the frequent sight of soldiers marching by. Both thrilled to the martial airs which were pounded out by the inevitable military bands. Between the King and the young Prince a bond of love was established. It was far more real than anything Wilhelm felt for his parents.

Undoubtedly the proudest moment in the youngster's early life occurred on his tenth birthday, 27th January, 1869, when he was given a commission in the Prussian army. At the same time, he was presented with the Exalted Order of the Black Eagle.

Above Wilhelm aged ten in the uniform of a guards officer in the Prussian army.

3 Prussia Marches

PRUSSIA WAS ON THE MARCH. In January 1864, the nation had flexed its military muscles by helping itself, with assistance from Austria, to the states of Schleswig and Holstein. Both had been governed by the King of Denmark since 1490, so the German claim to them was somewhat flimsy. The man who masterminded the affair was Prince Bismarck.

The war was brief. The Danes collapsed and Prussia was the richer by two states. As an added bonus, she had secured a neck of land through which the Kiel Canal could later be thrust—giving Germany a short cut betweeen the Baltic ports and the North Sea.

Bismarck was now playing a devious game of political chess. His object was to bring together all the German states under the leadership of Prussia. The way to do this, he decided, was war. In the heat of hostilities, he might weld the weaker to the stronger. Furthermore, by convincing victories, he would leave the world in no doubt about his country's place in the scheme of things.

Having dealt with the question of Schleswig-Holstein, he now turned to the problem of Austria. The Austro-Hungarian empire already controlled a large piece of central and south-east Europe. It might well consider itself the head of a unified Germany. Any such ideas must be reduced to the ashes of forlorn hopes. War with Austria was essential, but Bismarck was far too shrewd to attack first. Using an obscure argument which is not worth recounting, but which arose from the Schleswig-Holstein affair, he provoked Austria into mobilizing her forces in 1866.

> "Only three people have ever really understood the Schleswig-Holstein qestion—the Prince Consort, who is dead—a German professor, who has gone mad—and I, who have forgotten all about it." *Lord Palmerston.*

Opposite An incident in the Schleswig-Holstein War of 1864.

Italy sided with Prussia. Its government was anxious to regain Venice, which was currently under Austrian rule. So did the north German states. Bavaria and Württemberg took the part of Austria, but they produced little for the comfort of the embattled empire. The war was over in seven weeks. The military bands played triumphal music in Berlin. Wilhelm I and Bismarck opened yet another bottle of champagne.

The Chancellor now turned his attention to France. By conquering that country, he could secure the emerging Germany's western frontier. And, in the process, he might succeed in scooping Württemberg and Bavaria into the bag.

The prelude to the Franco-Prussian War showed the German Chancellor at his most brilliant. He proposed that Wilhelm's distant relative, Prince Leopold of Hohenzollern-Signaringen, should take over the throne of Spain. As a result, France would be sandwiched between Germany on one side, and a Prussian-controlled Spain on the other. It was not a prospect to be tolerated. Inevitably, stories of Bismarck's wheeler-dealing reached Paris, and the telegraph lines between the French capital and the embassy in Berlin became busy. The ambassador was instructed to find out immediately whether there was any truth in them. The logical person to deny or confirm them was King Wilhelm I.

Wilhelm was unwell at the time, and he had taken himself off to the spa at Ems to sip the healing waters. The ambassador accosted him as he was taking a brief constitutional along the promenade. After a suitable exchange of formalities, he posed his question with a directness that, under the circumstances, may have been less than tactful. The old King, no doubt thinking more about his health than about the worries of this excited diplomat, declined to comment. Nor was he prepared to promise his unwelcome intruder a further interview. He telegraphed a brief account of the meeting to Bismarck. As reported by the King, it was a matter of no importance.

But the Chancellor was editor as well as statesman. With a few deft touches, he reworded the telegram to make it seem as if the ambassador had been sent packing with a severe rebuff. Then he published his revised text.

When the French people read about it, they demanded war with Prussia—which was just what Bismarck had hoped for—and Napoleon III and his government responded to popular outrage. In July 1870, French troops marched against what, as soon became uncomfortably clear, now amounted to the *whole* of Germany. Once again, Bismarck's scheming had paid off.

The German forces swept aside the opposition and thrust into France. On an icecold day in January 1871, King Wilhelm I travelled to Versailles to be proclaimed Kaiser (Emperor) of Germany. Those who listened carefully could hear the crunch of Prussian shells falling on Paris in the distance. And back in Berlin, the young Prince Wilhelm waited impatiently for his grandfather's return. He wished to be the first to congratulate the old man.

> **"Place in the hands of the King of Prussia the strongest possible military power, then he will be able to carry out the policy you wish; this policy cannot succeed through speeches, and festivals, and songs, it can only be carried out through blood and iron."**
> *Bismarck, speaking in the Prussian House of Deputies.*

Below Wilhelm I proclaimed Kaiser of Germany at Versailles in 1871. Fritz stands behind him on the dais and Bismarck, in the light uniform, looks suitably proud.

4 The Way to the Throne

NO ALLOWANCES WERE TO BE MADE: the upbringing of the future Kaiser was to be entirely normal. After the death of Sigismund, when Wilhelm was seven, the Crown Princess's efforts intensified until they were not far short of brutal. Apart from this, her energies were devoted to infecting Germany with English liberalism, and doing what she could—which was not very much— to oppose Prince Bismarck. Her husband had a somewhat hazy idea of constitutional monarchy, and he trailed along meekly in the wake of her ideas—neither denying them nor adopting them. He had fought with some distinction in the Franco-Prussian War. He was less inclined to bear arms against his dominating wife.

And so young Wilhelm was sent to school. The grammar school at Kassel was chosen as a suitable place for the education of such an exalted mind. Inevitably, Hinzpeter was to accompany him with the object of supervising his academic studies. An army officer was detailed to look after his military education. His younger brother, Prince Henry, made up the party.

To begin with there had been some doubts about sending a future ruler of Germany to such an establishment. As a member of a class, sitting on the same bench as his schoolfellows, the highest child in the realm might be exposed to criticism. After all, why should he, who was beyond competition, have to compete? Understandably, both the masters and the other pupils felt uncomfortable at first.

Nevertheless the idea had its advantages. As Hinzpeter observed, it was "of the very greatest advantage

> **"On 27th January, 1859, a human being was born with an exceptionally strongly marked individuality which has developed according to its own laws, basically unchanged by anything and resistant even to the strongest external influences—a personality of a peculiar crystalline construction which has remained the same through all phases of development and has retained its own character through all the natural metamorphoses."**
> *Dr George Hinzpeter, on the development of Wilhelm's character.*

Opposite Wilhelm's mother guiding his studies. She was so strict that Wilhelm thought she hated him.

23

Above Wilhelm the schoolboy.

to the successful sovereign, ruler of a people, that he should know and understand their thoughts and feelings, and this is only possible if he has had the same method of education". In terms of human relationships, it certainly gave Wilhelm the edge on his grandfather and Bismarck, neither of whom had ever strayed far from the iron-edged world of the nobility.

As at home, the routine was one of work, work and more work. His studies kept him busy for more than twelve hours a day—with a short break for exercise. Writing about his schooldays in 1925, he observed: "It is a good thing that boys of the present day do not have such a hard time, for our life was often a perfect torment." Once, after a visit to the English public school at Eton, he came to the conclusion that the German system was altogether wrong. "The young Britons", he wrote, "have learned much less Latin and Greek, but they were inspired with the idea of making Great Britain still greater and stronger."

Greatness and strength were everything and, in the mind of Wilhelm, these virtues were personified by his grandfather. Wilhelm seems to have got on reasonably well with the boys at school, but there were no real friendships. Indeed everything suggests that at this period of his life he was intensely lonely. And, like many lonely people, he had a hunger for praise.

He could expect nothing of the kind from his parents. He must have suspected that his mother's impatience had infected his father. For Fritz was worried—even bitter—about the intellectual development of his heir. As he told a guest at Wilhelm's coming-of-age party, "Don't congratulate me ... my son will never mature, will never come of age." It was a harsh and rather unjust verdict.

Wilhelm I was first and foremost a soldier. For young Wilhelm, a soldier's occupation was the only one worth following. When he left the school at Kassel in 1877, he was attached to the 1st Guards Regiment as a lieutenant. His term of duty lasted for six months, and he loved every moment. But the process of education was not yet complete. In October of that year he was packed off to the university at Bonn, where he read law and national economics. By his own account, this was another period of hard work, enlivened by the sport of fencing (but never duelling). Other students might be tempted by frivolity, but it became a prince of the royal blood to be more serious.

"The dark side of student life", he recorded primly, "is undeniably its heavy drinking. I tried hard to check this pernicious habit [in others] while I was there, and even after I had left." Greater attention to sport, he hoped, would be the answer.

In fact, contrary to Wilhelm's own account of this period, he did not devote his time entirely to study. He had become infatuated with Princess Elizabeth of Hesse. He paid frequent visits to her parents' house, and wrote her innumerable and very bad poems. Elizabeth, who was only fourteen at the time, felt not the slightest flutterings of her own heart—indeed, she rather disliked him. He was a bad loser at tennis and a creature of sudden whims, which all the younger members of the household had to obey. When he tired of games or riding, he compelled them to sit quietly while, with Teutonic earnestness, he read aloud long passages from the Bible. It was all too much.

After Bonn, Wilhelm returned to his military career. The demands on his talents were not very great and he did well. He also developed a growing attachment for Prince Bismarck. On several occasions, he was a guest at the Chancellor's vast country house at Sachsenwald. Occasionally, he was given the rare privilege of being permitted to light the great man's pipe. It may appear to have been a somewhat servile act for a prince of royal blood; but Bismarck had put himself above royalty.

In 1879 his heart had presumably recovered from its ill-treatment by Princess Elizabeth. He began to pay court to Princess Augusta Victoria, daughter of Duke Frederick von Schleswig-Holstein. Since the Prussians had invaded Schleswig-Holstein and taken it by the sword, the Duke might have opposed the match. But,

Above Wilhelm the undergraduate.

25

Right The wedding of Wilhelm and Augusta Victoria in Berlin, 1881. They had six sons and one daughter. Wilhelm was often bored by his wife, who was neither clever nor beautiful.

"I think he may stand next to beloved Papa, and he is a person in whose judgement I would have complete confidence. I think him very fascinating, and (as in beloved Papa's case) so wonderfully handsome." *Queen Victoria, on Prince Alexander of Bulgaria, who nearly married Wilhelm's sister.*

on the contrary, he approved. The engagement should have been announced in January of the next year. Owing to the sudden death of the Duke, it was postponed until the following month. The couple were married on 27th February, 1881. Wilhelm was serving as a captain in the royal bodyguard at the time.

One year after his own romance had ripened into marriage, Wilhelm successfully demolished the hopes of his sister, Victoria.

The young Princess had fallen in love with Prince Alexander of Battenberg, who (with Russian sponsorship) was ruling Bulgaria. But Prince Alexander's independent ideas were worrying his Russian masters. They began to regret their choice. Indeed, they were wondering which would be better—to depose him or to arrange his assassination!

If Victoria were allowed to marry her handsome suitor, Germany's relations with Russia would obviously suffer. Furthermore, Prince Alexander was not entirely of royal blood—his mother came from a middle-class Polish family. Somebody would have to put a stop to this nonsense!

The British royal family were agreeable to the match and so was Wilhelm's mother. As for the docile Fritz, he did whatever his wife told him. It was therefore left to Wilhelm to step in—with Bismarck's prodding. He told the Prince and Princess that they must see no more of each other, and they obeyed him. Eventually, Prince Alexander abdicated.

In later years, Wilhelm piously noted: "It was a great grief to me that this cast a heavy shadow over my relations with my mother, and I also took the personal fate of my sister very much to heart. But as the well-being of the Fatherland was at stake, all personal desires had to be silenced."

What really happened was that Bismarck had asked Wilhelm to attend the coming-of-age party of the heir to the Russian throne. One of his duties had been to reassure the Tsar about Germany's opposition to the match. The assignment was taken to be a deliberate slight to his father (who might reasonably have expected to attend). Fritz was quick to voice his disapproval. "In view of the immaturity and inexperience of my eldest son, and of his tendency to arrogance", he informed the Chancellor, "I must consider it positively dangerous to bring him into contact with foreign questions so soon."

Although Wilhelm was still a soldier, Bismarck was tending to involve him more and more in diplomacy— and he appears to have enjoyed it. In 1886, he asked to be allowed to work at the German foreign ministry under the Chancellor's son, Herbert. It had no effect on policy, but it gave the Prince useful experience in the art of government. Whether it increased his liking for the Bismarck family is another matter. He was struck by Herbert von Bismarck's "rudeness towards his subordinates". If Wilhelm was complaining about Herbert's arrogance, he might have taken the opportunity to examine himself in this respect! Nevertheless, the time was approaching when whatever faults he had would have to be accepted. Within a year or two, he would be Emperor of Germany. And, unlike, his grandfather, he was determined that nobody, not even Bismarck, should determine his policies for him.

"We cannot be too grateful to him. The Emperor is entirely taken up with him. He expressed himself about the Prince with affection and the highest appreciation. In my audience I made no progress in the transaction of business."
Herbert von Bismarck, writing to his father about Wilhelm's first visit to Russia.

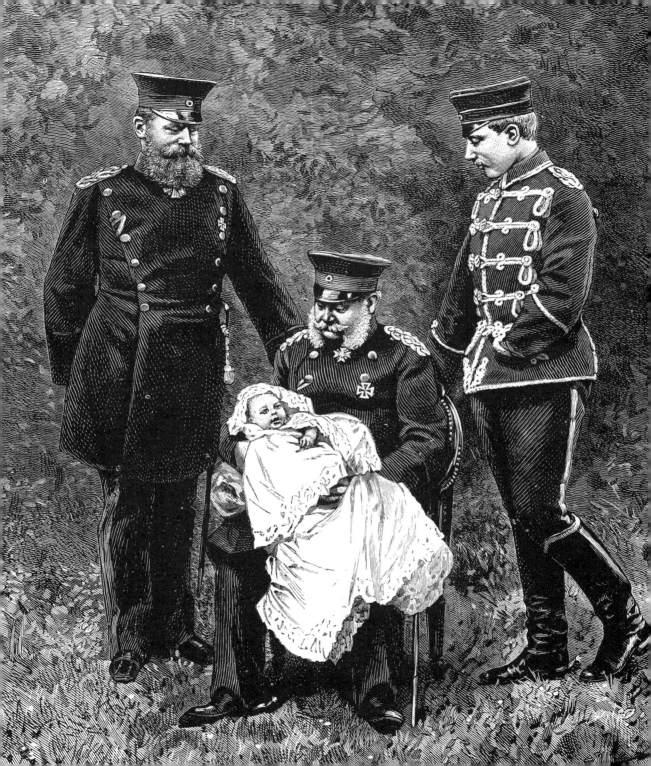

5 Hail to the Emperor

AT EIGHT O'CLOCK on the morning of 9th March, 1888, old Kaiser Wilhelm I died. One of his last actions had been to drink a glass of champagne. When he passed away, he was wearing a white jacket, and lying on a camp bed that had been with him on his military campaigns. His age was ninety-one.

His grandson was desolate. "I cannot express how deeply his loss affected me," he wrote, "not only as a grandson, but as a soldier. All I had become was due to him. Now that he was gone, I was robbed of my pattern and my guide."

The throne passed to Fritz, who became King Frederick III of Prussia, Emperor of Germany. But the new monarch was far from able to cope with his new responsibilities. In January of the previous year he had developed what seemed to be an infection of the throat. At first the doctors thought that it was the result of a number of colds. When a swelling was observed, a

> "Imagine feeling the magnificent German race bounding beneath you in ever swelling numbers, strength, wealth and ambition; and imagine on every side the thunderous tributes of crowd-loyalty and the skilled unceasing flattery of courtier adulation."
> *Winston Churchill, on Wilhelm II's background.*

Left The sarcophagus of Wilhelm I, the first Kaiser of Germany, at Charlottenburg.

Opposite Four generations of the Hohenzollerns—Wilhelm I, his son Fritz, his grandson (the future Wilhelm II) and his baby great-grandson, also called Wilhelm.

29

Above Sir Morell MacKenzie sitting contentedly in the garden while his patient, Kaiser Fritz dies of undiagnosed cancer.

surgeon tried to remove it by the agonizing application of a hot iron and tweezers. It became worse rather than better. Fritz was sent off to Ems for the cure. Again, there was no improvement.

A British laryngologist named Sir Morell MacKenzie was called in. The specialist said that the complaint was not cancer, as some had suspected. The condition would respond to a course of treatment. MacKenzie's diagnosis was hopelessly wrong and Wilhelm became suspicious. He had already conceived the idea that his mother was a British agent. Was the doctor part of the plot?

It was a crazy idea, but Wilhelm clung to it. Thirty-eight years later, when he might have been expected to take a more detached view of things, he was still capable of writing: "... the decisive proof is that, on the journey back to England after the death of my father, [MacKenzie] admitted that his only reason for not diagnosing the disease as cancer was that the poor Crown Prince should not be declared incapable of assuming the government!"

The truth is that before MacKenzie appeared on the scene, German doctors suspected that the cause was cancer and were prepared to operate. Had they done so, Fritz might have been reprieved. The British doctor's misplaced optimism had delayed the essential surgery. When at last he, too, became convinced, it was too late.

Frederick III ruled after a fashion for three months. For most of the time he was unable to speak and had to write everything down. His first action on coming to the throne was—typically, perhaps—to invest his wife with the Star of the Order of the Black Eagle. So far as more important decisions were concerned, the government of Germany was in the hands of Bismarck—with Wilhelm playing the role of watchdog.

"In fulfilment of my duty during this crisis", Wilhelm wrote, "I kept a watchful eye upon all happenings in military, official and social circles, and was inwardly outraged at the signs of slackness which I noted everywhere, and more especially at the hostility against my mother, which was becoming more and more noticeable."

His method of commenting on the situation was to scribble notes in the margins of documents. They were not very profound. Notes such as "Nonsense!" "Lies!" "Rascals!" and even "Stale Fish!" appeared. For those who hoped for a sane and responsible attitude to affairs of state, they provided little comfort.

Ninety-nine days after he had inherited the throne, Frederick III died. He was fifty-seven years old. Wilhelm's final words on his father were suitably tender. "Once more", he wrote, "he looked at us intently and lovingly with his kind blue eyes, and then he sank slowly back on to the pillows.... Quietly and without any death-struggle ... the second Kaiser of the new Germany breathed out his noble soul."

Apparently there was none of the sense of loss—desolation, almost—that Wilhelm had felt when that old war-horse, Wilhelm I, passed on to some heavenly palace.

Germany had a new Kaiser. Everybody, even Bismarck, waited uneasily to see what he would make of his responsibilities. Wilhelm—now Wilhelm II—was twenty-nine when he came to the throne. He had a thin face, bleak grey eyes, and light curly hair. Many people referred to his charm, though it is hard to find concrete examples. Nevertheless, there must have been more to him than the arrogant façade, which may have been a cover for insecurity.

His left arm remained weak and virtually useless. By contrast, his right had become abnormally strong. When shaking hands, he squeezed his unfortunate companion in a vice-like grip. To make the experience even more painful, he had a nasty habit of turning his rings round until they bit into the wretched man's flesh. What, then, is one to make of him? A bully? A sadist? A warlord who modelled himself on Attila the Hun?

When Queen Victoria died, Europe was ruled by four great emperors. Edward VII of England was the most outgoing of the four, the most powerful diplomat his

Above Kaiser Fritz's last conference with Bismarck.

"We have always been very intimate with our grandson ... and to pretend that he is to be treated *in private* as well as in public as 'His Imperial Majesty' is *perfect madness*. If he has *such* notions he had better *never* come *here*." *Queen Victoria, on the English royal family's relations with Wilhelm II.*

country possessed. Tsar Nicholas II of Russia was quiet and withdrawn; a gentle, almost tender man, whose fault was not brutality but ignorance about the conditions of his subjects. Franz Joseph of Austria was aged, aloof and (after his wife was assassinated in 1894) tragic. As for Wilhelm II, he was and perhaps always will be a puzzle.

On the one hand, he had been brought up by parents who disliked him, or so he supposed. On the other, he had been fawned upon and flattered as the future ruler of a new and mighty empire.

But Wilhelm's model was certainly not Attila the Hun. It was Frederick the Great—a man of ruthless power, but also a king who had cared for his people. When relaxing from affairs of state, Frederick had liked composing music and playing the flute.

Throughout his life, the new Kaiser found it difficult to make friends. There was only one person with whom he achieved anything approaching friendship. His name was Count Philip Eulenberg-Hertefeld.

Eulenberg had served in the army, but it had not taken him long to discover that he was unsuited to a military career. After a series of rows with his commanding officer, he resigned his commission and joined the diplomatic service. He was attached to the embassy at the Bavarian capital, Munich. (Bavaria did not become part of Germany until 1918.) His duties were light and he was able to indulge his passion for music.

It may, indeed, have been music which brought the ruler and the failed soldier together. Wilhelm admired his friend's compositions immoderately, and used to call him "the Nordic Bard". One piece especially appealed to him—*The Submerging of Atlantis*. It failed to achieve immortality, but Wilhelm said that he liked nothing better. The two men spent many happy evenings at the opera together. Like most Germans of the period, they had an unbounded enthusiasm for Wagner—and, above all operas, for *Parsifal*.

But the key to this unusual relationship lay deeper. Of all the people in Wilhelm's circle, Eulenberg was

32

most aware of his ruler's weakness. He realized instinctively the effect that Wilhelm's disability and his unfortunate upbringing had produced. He offered him compassion. And that, along with praise, was what Wilhelm desperately needed.

Next to Eulenberg, the new Kaiser's only friend was God. He believed that the Almighty was on his side, gently steering him in the right direction. It is easy to think of Wilhelm's assumption of divine authority as arrogance. But it may be more convincing to see it as the belief of a weak man clutching at hope. Fate had given him such huge responsibilities. And, if he was to believe his parents, he was totally unsuited to his role.

To everyone but Eulenberg, Wilhelm was an unpredictable man. For instance, after one of his frequent quarrels with his Uncle Edward, then Prince of Wales, relations between Britain and Germany moved into a state of tension. It was all the result of an unguarded remark Edward had made at Frederick III's funeral. Wilhelm was furious but eventually the whole thing was patched up by conferring on the new Kaiser the honorary British rank of Admiral of the Fleet. Wilhelm was delighted. He sailed for England with a collection of decrepit warships (the best Germany could muster at the time) and was effusive in his thanks.

For his mother, however, there was no forgiveness. On becoming Kaiser, his first act was to replace the staff at the palace, and to surround the building with troops. Nobody was to enter or leave the premises without a special pass. He then retired to his father's study, where he spent some time rummaging through the desk.

In his own memoirs, he closes the first volume before this incident—and opens the second one afterwards. Consequently, no-one knows what happened during this hour or so alone in his father's room. There were, however, two popular theories. One was that he was looking for a will which he suspected might benefit his mother. The other was that he was seeking evidence that she was, as he believed, an English agent. There is nothing to show that he came across either.

Above An engraving of Kaiser Bill's friend Count Philip Eulenberg-Hertefeld. The Count was a soldier and composer. He and Wilhelm shared a passion for music.

Above The famous *Punch* cartoon "Dropping the Pilot".

6 Dropping the Pilot

HIS GRANDFATHER WILHELM I had exercised the most influence over the new Kaiser. But Prince Otto von Bismarck had been a scarcely less powerful factor in his development. After all, he had carried out the task of ruling Germany. There had, admittedly, been a cabinet, a parliament (the Reichstag) and the other trappings of democracy; but these were little more than pretences. Bismarck was, for all practical purposes, a dictator.

The situation is admirably summed up by Lawrence Wilson in his book *The Incredible Kaiser*: "As long as Bismarck was at the helm there were no officers or even petty officers in the ship of state, but only anonymous galley-slaves straining every muscle to obey the master." Even the sovereign had obeyed in a sense— by giving almost blind approval to everything the Chancellor did.

When Wilhelm II came to the throne, Otto von Bismarck was seventy-three years old but he showed no signs of his advancing years. Since 1862, his rule had been absolute, and twenty-six years of much success and no opposition are intoxicating. No doubt he expected the new Emperor to be as compliant as his grandfather had been.

At first young Wilhelm seemed ready to conform to the pattern his Chancellor expected. He reviewed his troops and told them: "I believe that with God's help I have succeeded in preserving peace for many years to come." He made an unexpected visit to one of the great Atlantic liners in the service of North German Lloyd and made a suitably high-minded speech. He

> "Whatever the dark hours and the fog which may be in store for our Fatherland, our navy and our trade, we Germans will succeed in overcoming them, pressing strongly towards our goal on the principle: We Germans fear God, but no one else in the world." *Wilhelm II, in a speech made on board a transatlantic liner berthed in Hamburg.*

Opposite The Krupp steel works at Essen, scene of a strike in 1889. The workers are wearing heavy clogs and gloves but their hats look too soft for safety and their eyes are apparently uncovered.

was, Bismarck hoped, an adequate figurehead who was unlikely to meddle.

With his noble face and his large and heavily waxed moustache, the young Emperor cut a fine figure. But his first problems were not far away and they were to cloud the good relations which had always existed between him and Bismarck.

German industrialists flourished, but their wealth had its price. Whilst the men at the top enjoyed the good life in their sumptuous homes, their workers existed in conditions of appalling poverty. Young children were still employed, Sundays were treated just like any other working day, the workers had no say in things, and so on. It reflected the worst excesses of the Industrial Revolution in England, and marred the otherwise sunny face which Germany presented to the world.

Since Germany's development as an industrial power was about fifty years behind that of Britain, it was not surprising that concern for the welfare of workers also lagged behind. British factories were now producing more and yet their employees were putting in shorter hours than those in Germany. One reason for this was that Britain had more workers. Germany was primarily an agricultural community. The size of its army was another drain on manpower. But the real reason for the atrocious conditions was the inability of the ruling classes—industrialists included—to appreciate the point of view of their workers. They assumed that the lower orders would endure everything without complaint and keep to their place in society—even if it was horribly unjust.

Matters reached a head in May 1889 when, after fifteen years of industrial peace, the coal miners in Rhineland and Westphalia went on strike. They demanded higher wages and the reduction of their shifts from ten hours to eight hours. The strike spread to Essen, where the mighty Krupp armament works came to a standstill, and then reached out to include Saxony and Upper Silesia. At its peak, one hundred thousand workers were idle.

One of the Krupp family personally carried a long letter, its pages filled with anxiety, to Bismarck. The Chancellor read it, said that he felt like "an old circus horse" and did nothing. Other people were less sanguine. Without coal, Germany was powerless and there was an uneasy awareness of the Russians lurking beyond the eastern horizon. It would, as several soothsayers observed, be an admirable opportunity for the Tsar to pick a sudden quarrel and declare war.

In such circumstances, socialism flourished. In 1884 the Social Democrats polled only 550,000 votes. Three years later, the figure was 763,000 and in the year following the strike it dramatically doubled.

Bismarck's attitude was that socialism was one degree worse than liberalism (which, in itself, was bad enough) and that it must be stamped out. If repressive action resulted in Germany being plunged into civil war, the

Below A cheerful Socialist election meeting in Munich, 1890. The steins (lidded mugs) contain some of the city's famous beer.

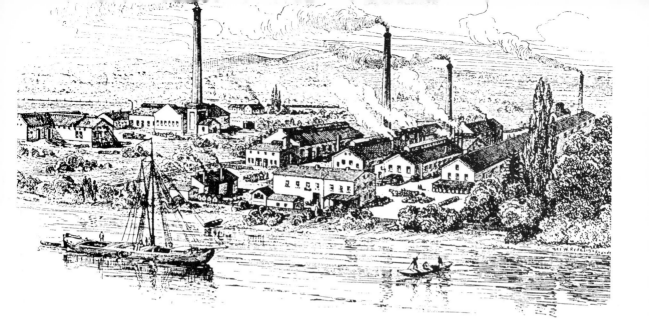

Above A German industrial scene, 1869.

Chancellor was unperturbed. He was sure that he was right and he had no doubt that might, in the shape of a well-drilled army, was behind him. Wilhelm, on the other hand, was less certain.

Taking Frederick the Great as his example, he was determined to rule *all* his people—with their consent. It might not be necessary for him to love them; but they must love him. Civil war was out of the question.

As was so often the case, the people at the top seemed to be unaware of what was happening at the bottom. Mine and factory owners were begging the military authorities to post sentries outside their office doors and officials were in a state bordering on panic. Meanwhile, the workers, whose demands were quite reasonable, were camping out peacefully on the hillsides.

Strangely enough, the Kaiser had a better understanding than most people of the realities. His old tutor, Hinzpeter, came from a mining district and, on one or two occasions, had taken his pupil into the pit workers' homes. As Wilhelm said: "I knew perfectly well that conditions among the labouring classes were bad and must be bettered at all costs."

"I wish to be a King of the rabble." *Frederick the Great.* "It was my duty to take care of those Germans who were exhausted by industry, to protect their strength and better their chances of existence." *Wilhelm II.*

In June 1889, the strike was settled and the Kaiser, always restless, set off on a long schedule of travelling. He visited one country after another until his subjects nicknamed him the *Reise Kaiser* (Travelling Emperor). But he had not forgotten the industrial unrest. When he returned to Berlin, he was full of ideas.

He was determined that the workers' pay should be increased, pregnant woman should not be employed in factories, Sunday working should be banned, industrial councils should be set up to attend to the workers' welfare, a special council of state (presided over by himself) should be convened to develop model coal mines and a European congress should be held in Berlin to study improved industrial conditions.

Bismarck was not receptive. His own idea was to take away the vote altogether in an attempt to halt the growing power of the Social Democrats! On one occasion, Wilhelm burst into a cabinet meeting wearing the uniform of an officer in the Hussars, and threatened to withdraw all military aid from the government unless his demands were met. The set of the Chancellor's mouth became even more stubborn.

In the elections which took place in February 1890, the Social Democrats polled 1,427,000 votes and won twenty-four seats in the Reichstag. Even Bismarck's own ministers, for so long his obedient lackeys, were now turning against him.

The Iron Chancellor was becoming more and more out of touch. He became indecisive, talked too much, and resolution gave way to the despair of the very lonely. Once, when everything seemed to be going against him, he was discovered on a sofa—crying his heart out. The adviser of princes, the designer of an empire, the politician whose intrigues were the work of a ruthless genius, was now an old and broken man. He had served his purpose; he could go.

Wilhelm was enjoying a musical evening with Count Eulenberg on 17th March, 1890, when he was called from the room. The letter he had been half-expecting, half-hoping for, had arrived. Bismarck had resigned. As the Count recalled, "Even in these painful hours his strange mercurial temperament did not desert him. Only for a few minutes was the music interrupted by the burning political question. The Kaiser was called out by the duty adjutant. When he returned and had sat down by the piano he whispered to me: 'The resignation has arrived'—then I had to go on singing."

But Wilhelm was not without regrets. "I feel as sorrowful as though I had lost my grandfather all over again." As for Bismarck's successor, Wilhelm had no doubt about what his lot would be. "Criticism, criticism, nothing but criticism—that was sure to be the daily bread upon which the new chancellor must reckon."

Below Keeping law and order in the Kaiser's Germany. The Cavalry put a stop to a Berlin riot in 1892.

7 Criticism, Criticism, Criticism

THE KAISER WAS A MAN of great enthusiasms. One was for his 28 hp Mercedes car. Historically, Wilhelm's adventures with automobiles may not amount to much. But in a way they tell us something about him and his methods.

He ruled very much as he drove. When the imperial car appeared on the roads, he insisted that everything else should get smartly out of its way. He even had a special horn designed, the notes of which seemed to spell out the announcement *Der Kai-ser Kommt* (*The Kaiser Comes*). Having warned people of his approach—and

Opposite Prince Chlodwic von Hohenlohe-Schillingfürst, one of Bismarck's most popular successors as Chancellor.

Below The Kaiser and his car.

having (he hoped) cleared the highway—he would work the vehicle up to a high, even reckless, speed. But then prudence took over. Suddenly losing his nerve, he would slow down. The danger was that in politics, as in motoring, he would one day apply the brakes too late.

Furthermore, in motoring as in so many other things, the Kaiser made mistakes. For example, that first imperial car was designed to be run on alcohol produced from potatoes. The idea was praiseworthy enough. If the fad took on and such fuel became an acceptable substitute for petrol, it would assure German farmers of another outlet for their crops. The trouble was that his theory had not been backed up by any research. When it came to putting it into practice, it turned out that motor vehicles ran very badly on this spirit!

Wilhelm replaced Bismarck with a mild-mannered, unambitious, former naval minister with an army background, General Count George von Caprivi. He had predicted that criticism would be the daily lot of this unfortunate individual and he meant it. What he omitted to say was that the bulk of it would come from Wilhelm himself. The rest would be delivered in a series of shattering broadsides by the Bismarcks, father and son.

At home, Wilhelm made it clear that there was to be "only one master in the Reich and that is myself. I will tolerate no other." He was going to tighten up Germany—to hunt out those responsible for the radical threat, to stamp out disloyalty and inefficiency. The villain of the piece, he said, was socialism. It must be rooted out at no matter what cost. This must have surprised those who had remarked on his earlier championship of the working classes!

The same message was delivered to a parade of recruits in Potsdam. "For you", he told them, "there is only one enemy and that is my enemy. In the present socialist conspiracies, it may be that I shall order you to shoot down your own relatives, brothers or even—which God forbid—your parents, but even then you must carry out my orders without complaint."

"Into battle for religion, morality and order against the parties of revolution. . . ! As the ivy clings to the gnarled oak and protects it while storms howl through its topmost branches, so the Prussian nobility gathers round my House. Let us enter this battle together! Forward with God! And dishonourable he who leaves his King in the lurch." *From a speech by Wilhelm II on his war against the radicals.*

Above Wilhelm reviewing the Guard, 1892.

It is doubtful whether he meant it (the Kaiser did not always *mean* what he said) but it shocked a good many of his subjects.

His instructions to Caprivi were uncompromising. The Chancellor was to introduce new laws very much along the lines of those thought out by Bismarck. These would deny the vote to a large proportion of the community and provide for overcoming opposition by force if necessary.

Caprivi urged caution. The Kaiser said "No". Caprivi offered to resign. The Kaiser said "Don't"—he'd had second thoughts. A speech he made one week later to Prussian landowners showed that he'd had nothing of the kind. Less than seven days after that, Caprivi was dismissed. It was impossible to say "Come back Bismarck, all is forgiven", and so Wilhelm did the next best thing. He appointed an elder statesman, until recently governor of Alsace-Lorraine, as Chancellor. His name was Prince Chlodwic von Hohenlohe-Schillingfürst. Bismarck approved of him and the Kaiser showed his respect for Hohenlohe's years and wisdom by addressing him as "Uncle".

Wilhelm's attitude to foreign policy was largely emotional. He had come to mistrust Russia when, a few

> **"William the Great** [Wilhelm II] **needs to learn that he is living at the end of the nineteenth century and not in the Middle Ages."** *Edward VII, when Prince of Wales.*

days before his resignation, Bismarck had let him see a letter from the Tsar. It referred to one of his visits to that country—a visit which the Kaiser had assumed to be a great success. The Tsar, apparently, was less enthusiastic. He referred to his guest as "a badly brought up boy and of bad faith".

No doubt he remembered these words when a treaty made by Bismarck with the Russians in 1887 came up for renewal in 1890. The idea behind it was that each power should look with friendly neutrality upon the misdeeds of the other—unless Germany attacked France, or Russia attacked Austria. It was known as the Reinsurance Treaty, and Wilhelm's foreign affairs advisers suggested that it should be abolished. As they pointed out, it permitted Russia to occupy Bulgaria—and this was entirely against the spirit of another treaty, signed in 1883, between Germany, Austria and Rumania. The Kaiser agreed. The last remaining strands of friendship between Germany and Russia were broken. Russia was more or less pitchforked into the arms of France. As for Germany, her only allies were now Austro-Hungary and Italy. Neither was to be relied upon.

Bismarck would never have approved. In the event of war, Germany was now liable to find herself fighting on two fronts. And that, as the Iron Chancellor had never tired of pointing out, was not the way to win victories.

Wilhelm's relations with England were curiously unstable. One moment, the Kaiser was being made an honorary colonel (much to his delight) of a cavalry regiment or an admiral of the fleet. The next, he was in disgrace. Much depended on the mood of his grandmother—and, of course, upon his own conduct.

During the early part of his reign, the prelude to the Boer War stretched relations between the two countries to very near breaking point. The Kaiser—and most of Germany, come to that—had worked out that the inhabitants of the Transvaal were Dutchmen and, therefore, of Lower Saxon-German origin. Consequently, if any trouble should break out, they deserved German support.

The trouble came on 1st January, 1896, when a party of raiding horsemen under the leadership of a Dr Jameson were soundly thrashed by President Kruger's men outside Johannesburg. Yielding to popular demand, Wilhelm promptly signed a telegram of congratulations to the Boer President: "I send you my sincere congratulations that without calling on the help of friendly powers you and your people have succeeded by your own efforts in restoring peace in face of the armed bands which have invaded your country and in preserving its independence against outside attacks."

It was noticeable that Wilhelm's signature on the document was not accompanied by that of his Chancellor. Indeed, Hohenlohe had a good deal of difficulty in persuading his master not to dispatch an adjutant to the Boer President, offering him German aid.

So long as Queen Victoria was on the throne, such episodes could be kept under control. When Her Majesty expressed her stern disapproval of her grandson's action, the latter wrote her a letter which, though it failed to fool the Queen, was a masterpiece of double-think. What he had *meant*, the Kaiser insisted, was that Jameson and his men were rebels: "rebels against the will of Her Most Gracious Majesty are the most execrable [abominable] beings in the world". Was anything wrong in that?

During the war itself, German opinion continued its pendulum motion. One moment a German newspaper was publishing a cartoon of Queen Victoria presenting the VC to a British soldier who had just raped a Boer woman. The next the Kaiser was offering fatherly advice on how to win a victory. Britain, he decided, needed larger forces more effectively deployed—plus, predictably, German friendship. Without these essentials, the game was lost. If that should happen, he pointed out, "even the best football club, if it is beaten despite the most gallant defence, finally accepts defeat with a good grace".

Above Dr Jameson's men after their unsuccessful raid, 1896. The plan had been to help foreign miners revolt against their Boer masters. But many thought it was an excuse to make more of South Africa British.

8 The World Beyond Europe

THE MOST SURPRISING THING ABOUT the new Germany was the speed at which everything had seemed to fall into place. The union of German states dated back only to 1871. And yet by the turn of the century Germany was not simply a major European power—she had an overseas empire as well. On a map of the world, the possessions might seem small and without very much significance. They certainly compared poorly with the large splodges of red ink which marked the British colonies. Nevertheless, they were sufficient to whet the Kaiser's appetite for more.

Wilhelm himself could take small credit for these distant possessions. Most of the work had been done as usual by Bismarck, but grudgingly. The ex-Chancellor may have been a boastful nationalist whose dreams for Germany were almost as large as his own ego. Nevertheless, he was a realist. There were problems enough in Europe to keep him busy. In any case, how could Germany hope to become a major colonial power, without a good navy?

The first people to carry German culture beyond the seas were the big commercial houses of Hamburg and Bremen. In Africa and the Pacific, a German military presence was later established to protect their interests. The operations were not carried out on any grandiose scale. When, for instance, the German colonization of Africa began in the mid-1880s, the spearhead was a small, ancient gunboat named the *Mowe*.

When Wilhelm came to the throne, he inherited German South West Africa, the Cameroons, Togoland and the north-eastern corner of New Guinea—plus a scattering of islands in the Pacific. The Bismarck archi-

"He very much likes to be talked about." *Edward VII on Wilhelm II's attitude to foreign policy.*

Opposite The German navy in action during the Boxer Rebellion, 1900. The Chinese rebels were called Boxers because they belonged to the "Society of Harmonious Fists".

49

Above A German expedition departing for the interior of South-East Africa.

pelago (three large and several small slices of land off New Guinea) and German East Africa followed in 1890, and there things seemed likely to remain.

But the Kaiser was not content. He was anxious to spread his cloak of power over any corner of the earth that was not already occupied by somebody else. Since his fleet consisted of seven battleships, a couple of cruisers and some small stuff, his naval assets could hardly be considered worthy of empire building. Nevertheless, this did not deter him.

The Far East particularly attracted him. Britain had Hong Kong, which was an important trading post and coaling station for British ships. He wanted something similar.

In 1894, the Japanese declared war on China. Their forces cut through the resistance like a knife through soft butter. By the spring of the following year, it was all over. The Emperor of Japan was delighted, the Tsar of Russia less so.

In that same year Alexander III of Russia died. He was the one who had written such unkind things about the Kaiser. His successor was Wilhelm's cousin Nicholas II, a shy young man who might be more pliable than his father. Russia's only outlet to the Pacific was Vladivostok, a bleak and unsatisfactory outpost which was icebound for three months of the year. The Russians needed Port Arthur (now Lushun), which was in a more temperate climate

So when the Japanese and Chinese discussed a peace treaty, the Tsar demanded that Japan should content herself with such small items as the island of Formosa. She must keep her hands off the Chinese mainland. Nicholas was extremely gratified when the Kaiser backed him.

It suited Wilhelm's interests too. He believed Japan needed to be kept in her place. That country was too efficient by half, and he did not want any interference with his own plans for conquest in the Far East. Furthermore, if Russia was occupied in that area, it would take the pressure off Germany's eastern frontier.

He egged Russia on. "Clearly", he wrote to Nicholas, "it is the great task for the future of Russia to cultivate the Asian continent and to defend Europe from the inroads of the Great Yellow Race. In this you will always find me on your side, ready to help you as best I can." He sent the Tsar an allegorical painting of the two monarchs with battleships in the background, and caused reproductions of it to be displayed on board all the Hamburg-America Line ships trading to the east.

But Wilhelm still did not have his German version of Hong Kong. At first, there was talk of annexing a port on the Chinese mainland opposite Formosa. But then on 1st November, 1897, the Chinese themselves played into his hands.

For some time the Germans had been trying to purchase the port of Tsingtau in the mineral-rich province of Shantung. The only response from the Chinese had been to dispatch more soldiers to the area. On the fateful day in question, two German missionaries were slaughtered there. This was all that Wilhelm needed. "I am now firmly determined to abandon our hypercautious policy which is looked on as weak throughout the Far East and to teach the Chinese with the utmost firmness and, if need be, with the most brutal ruthlessness that the German Kaiser will not allow himself to be joked with."

A squadron of German ships—led by the Kaiser's brother, Prince Henry, in the cruiser *Deutschland*—steamed into the port. They disgorged troops, who took the place by storm. Shortly afterwards, the German and Chinese governments negotiated a ninety-nine year lease; and, shortly after *that*, the Russians quietly took over Port Arthur. Wilhelm was happy. He now had his Hong Kong.

The trouble with Wilhelm was that he wanted a finger in every pie. In 1900 Chinese rebels (the Boxers) besieged the embassy quarter of Peking and murdered the German minister. He insisted on sending troops and ships, and urged that the relief expedition should be led by a German general.

"No mercy will be shown. No prisoners will be taken. As a thousand years ago the Huns under King Attila made a name for themselves still powerfully preserved in tradition and legend, so through you may the name 'German' be stamped on China for a thousand years so that never again may a Chinese dare to look askance at a German." *Speech by Wilhelm II to troops departing for China.*

"We must try to tie Russia down in East Asia so that she pays less attention to Europe and the Near East." *Wilhelm II to Chancellor Hohenlohe.*

9 Appointment in Tangier

THE BEGINNING OF THE TWENTIETH CENTURY saw the resignation of "Uncle" Hohenlohe. The old gentleman professed to be past handling the arduous duties of chancellor. Nor had he enjoyed addressing the Reichstag. In this respect, Wilhelm sympathized with him. One suspects that if he had been able to, Wilhelm would have abolished his parliament altogether!

Prince Hohenlohe went; Prince Bernhard von Bülow took his place. Wilhelm was pleased with his new Chancellor. A more fluent speechmaker, he was able to achieve some sort of parliamentary unity. He had previously been Secretary of State for Foreign Affairs, which gave him the necessary background of knowledge. And he was younger than any of his predecessors had been—consequently he was better able to stay the course.

In January 1901 Queen Victoria died. Wilhelm attended her deathbed. In his own account of the occasion, he was more concerned to describe the treatment he received in London than to show grief for an old lady who had frequently pulled him out of trouble without too much loss of face. Other people slept less easily. With nobody else able to bring her difficult grandson obediently to heel, what would become of the world?

In the same year his mother died. Her last wish was to be buried naked, covered only by a Union Jack. Wilhelm brusquely forbade it.

The years passed. In 1904 Russia declared war on Japan. She was roundly thrashed, having sent her fleet on an almost interminable journey from the Baltic to the Far East. While passing down the North Sea some

> **"The most mischievous and uncalled for event which the German Emperor has ever been engaged in since he came to the Throne."** *Edward VII, on Wilhelm's visit to Tangier.*

Opposite Kaiser Bill in the uniform of the Death's Head Hussars, 1900.

idiot opened fire on British fishing boats in the region
of the Dogger Bank. His excuse was that he had mis-
taken them for Japanese torpedo boats! The result was
tension between Britain and Russia—a state of affairs
Wilhelm was only too happy to encourage. He
promptly offered help to the Tsar if the outcome happened to be war. Nicholas II was grateful and agreed
to a meeting off the Finnish Island of Björkö.

Wilhelm was wild with excitement. He was playing
his game of being a self-appointed diplomat—a task
which he usually bungled but which appealed enorm-
ously to his vanity.

On this occasion, he felt that he was being un-
commonly shrewd. The proposed Russian text for a
treaty stipulated that the two powers should help each
other if either found itself in combat anywhere, on land
or sea, *in whatever part of the world*. Since Germany was
still without a fleet worthy of the name, this was clearly
impossible. Wilhelm crossed the clause out, and substi-
tuted *in Europe*. The Tsar agreed.

> **"The hours I was allowed to
> spend in your society will be
> ever graven in my memory, you
> were like a dear brother to me."**
> *Wilhelm II to Nicholas II after the
> meeting off Björkö.*

Above The Kaiser and his cousin Tsar Nicholas II of Russia.

But when the Kaiser triumphantly telegraphed news of the pact to Bülow, the Chancellor was less than enthusiastic. What good could it possibly do Germany? If Germany was involved in war with England, how could Russia help? By attacking India? Impossible— and, furthermore, ruled out completely by the words *in Europe*. Bülow tendered his resignation.

He received an almost tearful letter from the Kaiser. "If Bismarck had succeeded in extracting either of these assurances from Alexander I or Alexander II", Wilhelm wrote, "he would have been beside himself with joy ... I thought I had laboured for you and won an exceptional victory, and you send me a few tepid lines and your resignation!!!

"I am completely prostrated, and fear that I am on the verge of a nervous collapse ... I appeal to your friendship for me and beg you to let me hear no more of your intention to resign."

Bülow complied. It wasn't Wilhelm's first diplomatic blunder in 1905. Earlier, Britain and France had come to an accommodation over their affairs in North Africa. Britain was to turn a blind eye to France's determination to take over control of Morocco, and France was not to interfere in British dealings with Egypt. Nobody had asked Wilhelm's permission, which hurt. Bülow was worried. Somehow, the German presence must be felt, if only to disrupt the growing understanding which seemed to be developing between Britain and France.

Since he was unable to send a gunboat, Bülow decided to send the Kaiser. Wilhelm was about to depart for a holiday in Naples in a liner named *Hamburg*. Might he not, Bülow suggested, stop off at Tangier on the way and assure the Sultan of German goodwill?

At first, the Kaiser declined. "It seemed to me", he recalled, "that the Morocco question was too full of explosive matter." Eventually, however, he gave in "with a heavy heart".

What should have been a demonstration of German majesty went off like a piece of comic opera. The *Hamburg* had difficulty in berthing at Tangier. The journey ashore in a small boat was unpleasantly rough. There were few people on shore to greet the Kaiser—and most

Right A dismal Moroccan welcome for the Kaiser in 1905. The Sultan's uncle shakes his hand on the flag-decked pier.

of those who *were* seem to have been Spanish anarchists. The Moroccan troops got all their salutes wrong, and the speech—which was suitably full of references to German recognition for the Sultan as ruler of an *independent* nation—was received politely if without rapture.

The Kaiser continued his voyage, uneasily aware that his worst forebodings were about to come true. He was right. Everybody seemed to attach far more importance to the episode than it warranted. The French were furious. The British supported France—indeed, the two countries drew even closer together. In the end, everybody got round the table for a long and tedious conference in the Spanish town of Algeciras. The result of it was that world affairs remained much as they had been before Wilhelm paid his visit to Tangier—with one small exception. Nobody now had a good word to say for Germany.

Largely due to the efforts of his wicked uncle Edward, now Edward VII, the Anglo-French love affair had ripened into a kind of marriage. In 1903, the negotiations that produced the so-called *Entente Cordiale* had begun. One year later, the statesmen of both countries put their signatures to a pact that resolved a host of differences from Newfoundland fishing rights to the ownership of Madagascar (Britain yielded it to France). To Wilhelm, it was all heartbreaking.

But that untiring diplomat, Kaiser Wilhelm II, was not yet done. In 1908, he made a bid to win British sympathy by causing an article to be printed in the *Daily Telegraph*. In what claimed to be an exclusive interview, he went on record as saying that "You English are mad, mad as March hares." "What", he wanted to know, "has come over you that you are so completely given over to suspicion unworthy of a great nation?" Afterwards he disclaimed responsibility, saying that passages which he had ordered to be deleted had not been struck out. But the damage was done. At no time since the publication of his telegram to President Kruger had the standing of Wilhelm and his Germany sunk so low in British public opinion.

"All I hope is that you will send a telegram to Paris that the English and French Fleets are one. We could have the German Fleet, the Kiel Canal, and Schleswig-Holstein within a fortnight." *Sir John Fisher (England's First Sea Lord) after the Tangier episode.*

10   The Tools of War

SUCCESSFUL WARFARE has three vital ingredients: a sound plan, enough materials, and a sufficiency of troops. War between Germany and France was perhaps inevitable after Bismarck helped his country to Alsace-Lorraine following his 1871 victory. France wanted the provinces back and her statesmen never ceased grumbling about them. Germans—particularly the Kaiser—thought this attitude unreasonable. But then the Kaiser thought anyone unreasonable who considered himself and the Fatherland less than perfect!

Germany had the ingredients to deal with France, but to deal with Britain—if Britain should ever need to be dealt with—required more. Britannia claimed to rule the waves, and in the early twentieth century there was nobody to dispute her naval sovereignty. Germany, least of all, was fit to lock sea forces in combat with the Royal Navy.

Wilhelm was unhappily aware of this fact. During the Boer War he had often reflected that a force of well-trained German troops could have pushed either the Boers or the British into the sea—and given him the empire he craved. The trouble was that there had been no means of getting the soldiers to South Africa.

History has a neat way of arranging the pieces on the international chess board. Admiral Sir John Fisher was appointed by the British government (or destiny—who knows?) to revitalize the Royal Navy. The Kaiser had an officer who, he felt sure, was just as good. His name was Alfred von Tirpitz. After a successful career at sea, Tirpitz became secretary to the German navy at the end of the nineteenth century.

> **"We are in bitter need of a strong German fleet."** *Wilhelm II, after launching a new battleship.*

Opposite Wilhelm II with his naval chiefs, Admiral von Tirpitz and Admiral Holtzendorff.

The Kaiser and Tirpitz were in complete agreement
that what Germany needed was warships. To be precise, she needed twelve battleships, ten heavy cruisers,
and twenty-three light cruisers. Before they could be
built, however, the money had to be provided. When
the naval bill was about to be presented to the Reichstag, there were doubts about whether it would be
passed. Germany, after all, was not a seafaring nation
and a big naval budget looked like preparation for a
war. The German politicians were not looking for
trouble.

Bülow, who was then Foreign Secretary, was given
the task of piloting the bill through these difficult
waters. With his own eloquence, and the coincidental
outbreak of the Boer War to assist him, he succeeded.
Wilhelm got his ships. He also reaped some of the

Below Edward VII on a visit to his
cousin the Kaiser.

harvest from the long-past conquest of Schleswig-Holstein. In 1895 the Kiel Canal (originally named the
Kaiser Wilhelm Canal) was opened. Germany now had
a link between the Baltic and the North Sea.

A deadly warship-building race between Germany
and Britain was under way. When Edward VII visited
Kiel on the invitation of his nephew in 1904, he was
suitably impressed by the display of growing German
might. But Britain, urged forward by Fisher, had a bigger and better weapon in the locker—HMS *Dreadnought*,
which came into service in 1906. Once *Dreadnought* had
been launched everything else became obsolete. She
had greater speed, greater firepower, and an altogether
better design than any previous man-of-war. The
moment he heard about it, the Kaiser, who loved anything technical, decided that Germany, too, should

Below HMS *Dreadnought*. Launched
in 1906, this ship was so successful
that the Kaiser ordered imitations
for his own navy.

build Dreadnoughts. Since no other country had them under construction, there was no doubt about whom he saw as the possible enemy.

In 1910, the two countries attempted to halt this dangerous and very expensive competition, but the talks degenerated into stupidity. England wanted to know whether Germany would protect India—to which Germany replied: would Britain be prepared to guarantee Alsace and Lorraine? It was all a waste of breath. The big ships continued to come off the slipways. The Kaiser was among those who hoped that the two fleets would never collide. He liked to play at war but he had little stomach for its reality. In any case, his feelings for Britain were a curious mixture of love and hate. He was, after all, half an Englishman.

But the conquest of France would not need ships. In 1892, a general named Count Alfred von Schlieffen had taken over as the imperial army's chief of general staff. Much of his time was spent working on a plan against the French, for Schlieffen had decided that German military success in Europe depended on eliminating France. Once the western boundaries had been secured, an attack on Russia could follow.

Between Germany and France there was a short, heavily-guarded frontier. Any frontal attack on it would be suicidal. Over to the west, however, lay Belgium. If the German forces poured through Belgium, rather as water goes through a funnel, they could fan out on the far side, sweep round to the east, and encircle Paris and the French army.

Schlieffen decided that 1904 would be the year to put his plan into effect and the Kaiser agreed with him. The Russians were all too evidently about to wage war on Japan, Britain was still smarting from the effects of the Boer War, and morale in the French army had been low since 1893, when Captain Alfred Dreyfus was wrongly accused of passing on military secrets and sent to prison on Devil's Island. Until he was exonerated in 1906, France was divided on the rightness of the charge and the sentence. Since Dreyfus was a Jew, the frame-

Left Captain Dreyfus. The English artist of this picture noted: "A guardsman tore off the gold lace, the buttons, the embroidery and the red bands on the dishonoured officer's uniform. His sword was snapped in two, and cast on the ground. He was then marched round the square as a last disgrace."

up was one of the twentieth century's earlier cases of anti-Semitism.

Taken by and large, there could hardly be a better opportunity. But then the Kaiser bungled it. As so often, his ministers had cause to wonder whether their country needed enemies so long as they had Wilhelm! On this occasion King Leopold of Belgium was paying a visit to Berlin. Before dinner on the last night, the Kaiser took him to one side. His proposition was that Leopold could more or less help himself to whatever pieces of France he liked—in return for an unimpeded passage by German soldiers. The Belgian King said that he was sure his ministers would never agree.

The Kaiser was pained. Conversation at dinner that night was small and everybody was relieved when the visiting monarch and his party took the train back to Brussels. The invasion of France did not take place.

By the time the Schlieffen plan was put into operation, its author was dead and France and Britain both knew all about it. The secret had been betrayed by a German officer at about the time Wilhelm was visiting Tangier.

"If, in a number of utterances, I admonished my people to 'keep their powder dry' and 'their sword sharp', the warning was addressed alike to friend and foe. I wished our foes to pause and think a long time before they dared to engage with us."
Wilhelm II.

63

11 From One Crisis to Another

EUROPE REELED UNDER CRISIS UPON CRISIS and no upheaval in this unhappy continent was complete without the voice of the Kaiser. One moment, His Imperial Majesty wanted war. That alone could furnish proof of his and Germany's greatness. The next—hurrying flustered from the brink—he seemed desperately concerned to preserve peace. Just what *did* he want? He appeared to be no more sure than anyone else.

In 1908 the apparently tireless Bülow finally ground to a halt. The trouble lay not beyond the German frontiers, but within. How was he to keep the Reichstag happy *and* satisfy his master?

Wilhelm wrote of the political climate: "Just as the Conservatives did not do enough out of respect for the Crown to satisfy me, so also the Liberals of the Left, the Democrats and the Socialists distinguished themselves by an outburst of fury, which became, in their partisan press, a veritable orgy, in which loud demands were made for the limitation of autocratic, despotic inclinations, etc. The agitation lasted the whole winter, without hindrance or objection from high government circles."

Bülow resigned and Wilhelm accepted his choice of a successor. The new Chancellor was to be Theobald von Bethmann Hollweg, a former Prussian minister of the interior. He was less assertive than Bülow—and less decisive. He seemed to be thoughtful, even cautious, and he knew nothing whatever about foreign affairs. That, in Wilhelm's opinion, was no disadvantage. He considered himself well able to guide his new man through the jungle.

The conference at Algeciras had taken the Moroccan

Opposite Wilhelm visiting King George V, who succeeded to the British throne on Edward VII's death in 1910.

question off the boil, but it had done little more. In 1911 the French made it clear that they proposed to take the country over completely. The Germans reacted in the traditional manner, by sending a gunboat (a ship named *Panther*) to Agadir. Officially it was assigned to protect the lives and property of German residents. But everybody assumed it meant far more than that.

In London, the government suspected it was the first step towards a permanent German military presence in Morocco. The statesmen also saw the danger of Europe becoming split into two camps, with France on one side and Germany on the other. France, of course, was furious. The strings of peace underwent further tension.

Eventually everything and everyone calmed down. Germany swapped a small piece of the German Cameroons, plus a pledge that France could do whatever she liked in Morocco, in return for a large chunk of comparatively worthless French Congo soil. The moral, so far as the Kaiser was concerned, seemed to be that an even bigger German fleet was needed. He instructed Tirpitz to build one super-battleship a year and over twenty more submarines. Tirpitz gleefully complied.

But more trouble was in store. The Ottoman Empire of Turkey had once been one of the world's great powers—stretching across North Africa and deep into Europe. During the past four decades, its power had waned. In 1829, the Turks had been driven out of Greece. After the Treaty of Berlin in 1878, they had been forced to abandon Serbia, Bulgaria and Rumania. Nevertheless, traces of Ottoman domination remained in Albania and Macedonia. Somehow these, too, had to be prized loose. In 1912, the armies of Serbia, Bulgaria and Greece were supported by Russia as they marched to war. No doubt they were also heartened by the Kaiser, who said that "if they smash the Turks, then they are in the right and are entitled to reward". They smashed the Turkish forces in a swift battle at Adrianople on 26th March, 1913. This should have satisfied everybody—except Turkey.

Above German submarines, called U-boats, short for "Untersee"
(undersea) boats.

Far from it. Russia was concerned lest Bulgaria should now take Constantinople and so command the entrances and exits to the Black Sea. Serbia wanted a port on the Adriatic. Austria, aware that there were seven million Slavs residing in Austro-Hungary, became concerned about the growing might of Serbia. And the Kaiser, worried about the security of Austria, wished he had kept his mouth shut.

Between crises, Wilhelm hunted in East Prussia; displayed himself aboard the royal yacht at the Kiel Regatta (a German version of Cowes); visited his house on Corfu, where he took an interest in archaeology; spent the summer cruising with his fleet in the Norwegian fjords; and generally enjoyed himself in his rumbustious manner.

His relations with his ministers followed a pattern. When they opposed him, he countered with anger. If that failed, he tried to coax them. And, when that was of no avail, he fell back on self-pity. One moment he was the supreme warrior, destined for the sanctuary of Nordic gods in Valhalla. The next, he was a snivelling small boy.

In this insecure world, there was little safety for a sovereign. In 1894 the President of France had been assassinated. The Empress of Austria had been done to death in 1898. Thereafter the King of Italy (1900), the King of Portugal (1908) and the King of Greece (1913) were all murdered.

The next fatal shot was fired on 28th June, 1914, at 10.40 on a Sunday morning. The place was Sarajevo. The victims were Wilhelm's old friends, Archduke Franz Ferdinand, heir to the Austrian throne, and his wife. The fateful bullets were fired by an incompetent schoolboy. If the arrangements for the royal visitors had not been badly managed, the assassination would have failed. In this supreme moment of history, the destiny of the world was controlled by a chauffeur. Because he had been badly briefed, he took the wrong turning—and delivered his precious freight within range of the young killer's pistol.

68

Top The Archduke just before he was shot.   *Below* Catching the assassin.   69

BRAVO, BELGIUM!

12 The Final Eruption

THE KAISER WAS ON BOARD his yacht at Kiel when he heard about the assassinations. He immediately cancelled the regatta which was about to take place. When he proposed to attend the funeral in Vienna, he was dissuaded from doing so by his Chancellor. "Later", Wilhelm wrote, "I heard that one of the reasons for this was consideration for my personal safety, to which, naturally, I would have paid no attention."

Austria was obviously going to exact a fearful penalty from Serbia for the death of the heir to the throne. Since Russia could be expected to come to Serbia's aid, a crisis of titanic proportions was in the making. From Kiel, the Kaiser was scheduled to sail for his annual cruise in the Norwegian fjords. This, too, he said, should be abandoned. Bethmann Hollweg disagreed. By cancelling the trip and hurrying to Berlin, His Imperial Majesty would be adding to the international tension. Wilhelm reluctantly agreed. He sailed for Norway.

During the next few days events moved at such speed that, looking back on it, it seems amazing that so much could be compressed into such a small capsule of time. When the Kaiser observed that the British fleet had not dispersed after its annual review at Spithead, he knew that, no matter what his ministers might say, the time had come to return. The German warships were concentrated at Wilhelmshaven. He himself went posthaste to Berlin, where he found that opinions were sharply divided. General Helmuth von Moltke, chief of the general staff, believed that war was inevitable. The foreign office thought otherwise and so, at first, did the Chancellor.

> "On 1st August Germany declared war on Russia; two days later, with hardly an attempt at excuse, on France. The First World War had begun—imposed on the statesmen of Europe by railway timetables. It was an unexpected climax to the railway age." *A J P Taylor, in* The First World War.

Opposite A *Punch* cartoon on the German invasion of Belgium, which brought Britain into the war.

As for Wilhelm, he was thoroughly confused. From the royal yacht, on the day following the assassination, he sent Nicholas II what seemed to be a helpful telegram. His concern was to prevent Russia from rushing to the aid of Serbia:

"It would be quite possible for Russia to remain a spectator of the Austro-Serbian conflict, without involving Europe in the most horrible war she ever witnessed. I think a direct understanding between your government and Vienna possible and desirable.... Of course, military measures on the part of Russia which would be looked upon by Austria as threatening, would precipitate a calamity we both wish to avoid, and jeopardize my position as mediator...."

The flow of telegrams between Wilhelm and Nicholas continued until, at last, Wilhelm wrote: "I have gone to the utmost limits of the possible in my efforts to save peace. It is not I who will bear the responsibility for the terrible disaster which now threatens the civilized world. You and you alone can still avert it."

But could he? And was there a scrap of justification for the Kaiser's words?

After the killing of Franz Ferdinand and his wife, Austria had handed Serbia an ultimatum. In the opinion of the British Foreign Secretary, Sir Edward Grey, he had "never seen one state address to another a document of so formidable a character". If Serbia accepted it, she would be signing away her independence. But Serbia did accept it (with one or two minor modifications)—and within the time limits.

But Austria was not content. The fact is that she had wanted to wage war with Serbia for some time. The killing of the Archduke had merely acted as an excuse. How then could Austria start a war? The answer was to occupy Belgrade, the Serbian capital, under the pretence of making sure that the terms of the ultimatum were carried out. The action fooled nobody—especially when Austrian guns began to bombard the city.

Russia was scandalized at this treatment of what the Tsar called "a weak country" and mobilized. In Russia, "mobilization" meant an advanced state of sabre-rattling. According to the Schlieffen Plan, however—which was old, but still considered ripe—"mobilization" meant war.

England's attitude was unclear. During a conversation with Wilhelm's brother, Prince Henry, King George V had said, "We shall try all we can to keep out of this and remain neutral." Wilhelm had assumed that it meant Britain had no intention of taking part—no doubt because he overlooked the word *try*. Consequently, it came as a rude shock to him when Sir Edward Grey (the Foreign Secretary) announced that if Germany and France were brought to battle, Britain might have to join in.

Wilhelm was outraged. He called Grey "a common cur" and the English "a common crew of shopkeepers". He suggested it was all a dark plot which had been hatched years ago by his wicked uncle, Edward VII. The question, of course, arose as to *why* Germany should attack France. Wasn't this just another Balkan squabble—more dangerous, certainly, than the others but still capable of being contained?

The precise reason why the First World War broke out, and the way in which hostilities began, is a question that has intrigued and sometimes baffled historians for more than half a century. France was pledged to assist Russia and Russia was protesting its loyalty to Serbia to the point of mobilization. In fact, this small Balkan state did not require any aid: it was perfectly willing to accept the Austrian demands, which did not seem to be unreasonable. But things had now gone far beyond a local dispute. If Russia, as seemed probable, was about to attack Austria, Germany would have to attack Russia—which meant, of course, that France would have to attack Germany. There seemed to be no reason why Britain should attack anyone at all.

By this time, Schlieffen had been dead for a good few years. Nevertheless, he had left behind two fragments of military philosophy that were to govern the Kaiser's thinking. The first was that it pays to deliver the first

Above Sir Edward Grey, the British Foreign Secretary. Wilhelm called him "a common cur".

"Slippery as an eel! Hypocritical liar!" *Wilhelm II about Sir Edward Grey, after war was declared.*

blow. The second was that a war should never be fought on two fronts. To begin with, Germany could march its armies either in the direction of Russia *or* towards France. On no account must it attempt to do both at the same time.

First thoughts suggested an initial offensive against Russia. But somebody may have remembered what happened when Napoleon turned his armies eastwards. The distances were too great and the project far too difficult. France seemed to be a more reasonable target, though nobody in his right mind can have expected the history of the Franco-Prussian war to repeat itself. The frontier was now guarded by a strongly-fortified line. If this could be bypassed, or so Wilhelm and his advisers believed, the rest would not be too difficult. The obvious way to do it was to march through Belgium.

The timetable was now as follows: On 28th July, Austria declared war on Serbia. On 1st August, mistaking Russian mobilization as a threat to her ally Austria, Germany declared war on Russia. And on 3rd August—as the first act in their campaign against Russia—Germany declared war on France.

But even at the very last moment Wilhelm had doubts. He asked Moltke if it really was necessary to fight France. Couldn't they turn eastwards instead of westwards and make straight for Russia? Moltke said it was impossible. The Schlieffen plan was the only one they had. If they tried improvizing alternatives at the last moment, the Kaiser "would no longer command an army, but a disorderly rabble".

Tearing up a document guaranteeing Belgian neutrality which Wilhelm now called a worthless "scrap of paper", the German army crossed the frontier into Belgium. For Britain, the violation of Belgium was the last straw. On 4th August, she declared war on Germany.

The so-called Great War had begun. Wilhelm was happy after his fashion. Germany, no matter what the earlier bickerings in the Reichstag may have suggested, was united. What was more, with 4,300,000 trained men in her army, plus another million half-trained, she was the most formidable fighting force in the world. As he said at the opening of the Reichstag that month, "I know parties no more; I know only Germans."

Below The Krupp works at Essen turning out armaments in 1914.

13 The Great Killing

THE SOUL OF SCHLIEFFEN must have been in torment. For over twenty years his master plan had lain on ice. Throughout this period nobody had thought to question its wisdom. It had been the root and branch of German military thinking, the Bible of attack. And yet when at last it was tried out, it turned out that Schlieffen had got it wrong. The almost instant victory over France he had predicted was impossible. The road through Belgium might be narrow, but beyond it there was far too much of France. And the Kaiser had told the British foreign minister that German troops could be in Paris within two weeks.

Schlieffen's plan had been thought up as a means of defeating Russia. Instead it led to a fullstop in the mud-caked fields of northern France. The armies dug themselves in; and, for four years, slaughtered each other in return for minute territorial gains.

And worst of all it was completely unnecessary. The Germans deployed a thin force to keep its eye on Russia in readiness for the big thrust. Admittedly, the Russians did succeed in penetrating into East Prussia, but then they were halted. At the Battle of Tannenberg ninety thousand Russian soldiers were taken prisoner. One of their two armies was virtually wiped out. The other was forced into retreat. And all this was accomplished while the cream of the German army was locked in a life-or-death struggle with France and Britain.

By 1917 Russia was preoccupied with the Bolshevik revolution. Once Lenin was given a safe conduct through Germany from Switzerland, the revolutionaries knocked their country out of the war without the assistance of a single German soldier.

> "The General Staff tells me nothing and asks me nothing. If people in Germany imagine that I lead the army they greatly deceive themselves. I drink tea, saw wood, go for walks and from time to time hear this or that had been done, just as the gentlemen choose." *Wilhelm II to Max von Baden.*

Opposite The Kaiser watching his troops in the trenches with General Helmuth von Moltke, chief of general staff.

As for Serbia, which was what it had all been about, that country was overwhelmed by Austria on 28th November, 1915.

In peace, the Kaiser had set himself up as the personification of German glory. He was more than a man, he was a symbol. Now the Germans saw him as symbolic of the death and misery in the trenches. His enemies portrayed him as the brutal warlord—the loathed serpent which had brought destruction to Europe.

Nobody saw him as a hero. Nobody seemed to need him. His government governed with little help from him. They seldom told him what they were doing. His generals never asked his advice. Even when he visited the front, his presence seemed to be an embarrassment. He prevented people from getting on with their jobs. He searched the faces of his soldiers in vain for any traces of the love and loyalty he expected.

Often in the daytime, he chopped wood. During the evenings he played cards. He became sullen and listless. This was not as he had dreamed it would be. In 1916, aided by Bethmann Hollweg, he wrote a letter offering to make peace. It was more or less ignored. When he approached the Pope on the matter, he was no more successful. Germany, like every other participant, had her victories and her defeats. For Wilhelm, the war was one long failure.

For much of the time, his country was divided by its own war of ideas. Bethmann Hollweg was of the opinion that the war *had* been a terrible mistake. The best thing would be to end it with as much dignity as possible.

The military took the opposite view. Early on, Moltke had been dismissed for incompetence. The man of the moment was a general named Erich von Ludendorff. But Ludendorff was too junior to hold the supreme office. Consequently, the elderly General Paul von Hindenburg was dug out of retirement. Hindenburg became chief of the general staff: Ludendorff became quartermaster general. The power of the two men—who believed in victory or total destruction, but nothing in between—exceeded that of the Kaiser.

Above General Paul von Hindenburg, Wilhelm and General Erich von Ludendorff studying a war map.

But Wilhelm kept up his illusions. He let it be known that Hindenburg never did a thing without consulting Ludendorff, and that Ludendorff received his advice from the throne. Nobody believed it any more than they believed in victories which, out of the kindness of the army's heart, were put down to the Kaiser's credit.

An ever-present anxiety was that the United States would declare war on Germany. It had been a possibility ever since a U-boat (submarine) captain had sunk the giant ocean liner *Lusitania* in 1915. Wilhelm was seldom lacking in imagination. This time he went beyond all bounds of reason. One day in early 1917, he ordered his Foreign Secretary to send a cable to the Mexican government. The moment, he said, was just right for them to attack the USA—with the object of recovering Texas, New Mexico and Arizona. As he pointed out to anyone who dared to be sceptical, if the Americans were

Above Rescuing survivors from the *Lusitania*, a passenger liner sunk by a German U-boat in 1915.

engaged in fighting at home, they would have neither the time nor the resources to join in a European war. Like so many of Wilhelm's bright ideas, it rebounded against him. The text was intercepted by the British and was promptly published throughout the USA. Naturally, opinion against Germany hardened—especially in Texas. Later that year, America did declare war against Germany—though the cause was the German U-boat commanders. Turning a blind eye to neutrality, they were still sinking American ships.

Throughout this period, Wilhelm's moods of in-activity were broken by spells of feverish bustling. Then the royal train would suddenly get up steam and Wilhelm would be off to the general headquarters in the Belgian town of Spa, or visiting the troops up at the front, or showing his imperial presence to the steel-workers at Essen. The best that could be said of these expeditions was that nobody threw an egg at him!

By 1917 matters were heading for a showdown in Germany. Ludendorff refused to have any more dealings with Bethmann Hollweg and his continued peace feelers. The Chancellor resigned and eventually a mousey middle-class Prussian named George Michaelis was appointed. He remained in office for a matter of months, then he was replaced by an older man called George Hertling. But Hertling did not stay very long either. In 1918, he was replaced by Wilhelm's cousin, Prince Max von Baden. By this time the Kaiser hardly cared who held the position.

The Kaiser saved his ink when it came to writing of the dead. In 1917, his cousin Tsar Nicholas II and his family were killed by the Bolsheviks at Ekaterinburg. In neither of the two volumes of memoirs he published after his abdication did he make more than a factual reference to the affair. He uttered no words of regret. This may have been because the soil of France was then drenched with the blood of his own people. But he did not seem to read any warning into what had happened. Since the Reichstag now had a strong left wing, he might have been worried. But Germany, no less than the Kaiser, was full of surprises. How else, when the country was near revolution, could a prince—even a *minor* prince—be made Chancellor?

In the spring of 1918, it seemed to Wilhelm that the tide of battle had at last turned. All along the front, the British and French troops were being pushed back. He was jubilant. Everything was going to be all right. The Allies might say that the only conditions under which they would consider peace were the giving up of Belgium, the return of Alsace-Lorraine to France and the surrendering of all other occupied territories. They might refuse to deal with the Kaiser and his generals, but who cared any more? Germany was going to *win*.

By July, the offensive had exhausted itself. The soldiers were tired and they were running out of reserves. The long march back was beginning. On 26th October, after long discussions with Ludendorff, the Kaiser left for the headquarters at Spa. The troops were in for another long spell on the defensive, and he proposed to take personal charge of their morale. The people in Berlin pleaded in vain that he should remain

"Just as no sacrifice in endurance and privation was too great for those who were at home, so also the army, in defending itself during the war so criminally forced upon us, did not merely overcome the crushing superiority of twenty-eight hostile nations, but on land and water, and in the air, won victories." *Wilhelm II.*

behind. He would not listen. This could be the moment that he, in his imagined role as the Prince of Glory, had been waiting for.

A new offensive was being planned for the navy, but it was two years since the German sailors had been in battle. They no longer had any stomach for the fight. When the seamen at Kiel were given their new orders, they mutinied. The trouble spread to other ports. Coming sullenly ashore, they broke up into bands and terrorized the north of Germany.

One by one, Germany's allies were crumbling in defeat. In September, Bulgaria capitulated, and in October the Turks followed suit. On 3rd November, the once-great Austro-Hungarian Empire finally hung out the white flag. Germany was all on her own, beaten and ripe for revolution. Six days later, a republic was proclaimed in Berlin. Two days afterwards, at five o'clock in the afternoon, a three-man German armistice commission, headed by a politician named Matthias Erzberger, went to a lonely railway carriage in the French forest of Compiègne. The peace terms were harsh, but Erzberger signed. The unnecessary war, which had cost so many millions of lives, was over.

Wilhelm's part in it had ended the day before. He was still at Spa—apparently oblivious to what was going on in Berlin. When he was told that he had been deposed, his first reaction was one of rage, then stubborness. He would not give in. He'd fight the war on his own. He would barricade himself at Spa, proclaim himself King of Prussia, return to Berlin and take the capital by the sword.

Alas, like so many of the Kaiser's dreams of glory, it all came to nothing. Wilhelm's career as Emperor of Germany was over. His only hope was to seek sanctuary in a neutral country. At five o'clock on the morning of 10th November, after a hold-up at the frontier, he was admitted to Holland. To attract as little attention as possible, he travelled by car. Since the Dutch government had expected him to arrive by train, there was no one to meet him.

Above The German party arrives at Compiègne to surrender.

PEACE TERMS
1919

14 The Years of Exile

FOR OVER FIVE HUNDRED YEARS a Hohenzollern had ruled in Germany. Now it was all over. The descendent of Frederick the Great was waiting on a rain-drenched railway platform in Holland, watched uneasily by Dutch frontier guards. From time to time, their distinguished guest looked impatiently down the track—searching for the first smudge of smoke which would herald the arrival of the imperial train from Spa. At last, after several hours, it appeared. On board were the thirty members of the Kaiser's suite (including six secretaries), innumerable pieces of baggage, and the inevitable crates of champagne.

Wilhelm climbed on board. His host for the time being was a Dutch count named Godard Bentinck. The Count had put his house in Amerongen at the Kaiser's disposal. With commendably quick improvization, the stables were already being converted into quarters for his staff. The royal refugee arrived there on the next day.

He was followed, some days later, by his wife, the Empress Augusta, who had been in Berlin throughout the final weeks. When the Kaiser had married her, she had been a laughing girl. Now she was a sick and broken woman, fussed over by two pious female retainers. She already had a serious heart condition and her husband did not exaggerate when he wrote: "The revolution broke the Empress's heart."

Germany was now a republic, governed by the Social Democrats and the Catholic Centre. The rulers styled themselves "The Council of the People's Commissioners" (it sounded more leftist than in fact it was). Nobody mourned the absence of poor Wilhelm.

"What a contrast twelve years would show! A broken man sits hunched in a railway carriage, hour after hour, at a Dutch frontier station awaiting permission to escape as a refugee from the execration of a people whose armies he has led through measureless sacrifices to measureless defeat, and whose conquests and treasures he has squandered." *Winston S Churchill in* Great Contemporaries.

Opposite The ghosts watching Kaiser Bill signing the peace treaty at Versailles are General von Moltke, Wilhelm I and Bismarck—the winning team in the Franco-Prussian War fifty years before.

Nevertheless, at Amerongen there was much to keep the exiled emperor busy. The press swarmed into Holland. At Versailles, where the peace treaty was being settled, his victors were eager for blood. "Hang the Kaiser" was the popular catch phrase—and most people meant it.

Delving into his copious memory, Wilhelm assembled evidence for his defence. Chopping down trees, going for long walks in the woods, smoking endlessly, he considered fact after fact. In the event, he was not to need it. The Dutch government had promised their guest sanctuary, and that was what he should have. They refused to hand him over.

Eventually, everything calmed down. In 1920, he bought a large house and 150 hectares (60 acres) at Doorn. Although an exile, he was still well off. The new government of Germany enabled him to receive the incomes from his large estates in the Fatherland. He maintained a sizeable staff and nine cars, and when the occasion seemed appropriate he still wore his field marshal's uniform.

In April 1921 the Empress died. One year later, he married the Princess Hermine of Reuss. His new wife was an uncomplicated widow aged thirty-four, who already had five children. Wilhelm did not add to the score.

The years rolled by. Wilhelm's life was quiet and peaceful, and he would not have had it otherwise. He now paid less attention to the meticulously turned-up ends of his moustache, and he had grown a small beard. Visitors found him an amiable old man who seemed, at last, to have discovered the importance of thinking before he spoke. At any rate, he never discussed German politics.

For some years he nourished the hope that Germany would discover what a terrible mistake she had made and beg him to return to the throne. Such dreams finally died when Hitler came to power. In his book, *Mein Kampf*, the Nazi dictator had remarked that the Kaiser was "obviously insane". He was unlikely to come crawling to the former emperor for help.

Above Wilhelm, driving near Amerongen, his first home in exile.

When the German forces overwhelmed Holland in 1940, the British government, long forgetful of the demand to "hang the Kaiser", offered their one-time enemy refuge. He was, after all, half English. He declined. The invading forces graced his residence with a guard of honour and droves of tourist came to look at him.

His last act was to plan his own funeral. He had ordered an imposing mausoleum to be built in the garden. At the service, there were to be no speeches, just the reading of a few carefully chosen passages from the Bible. On 4th June, 1941, he died. The bluster, the arrogance, and the pretences had gone. At the end, he was just a tired old man.

> **"Wilhelm II, German Emperor and King of Prussia. Died in exile 4th June, 1941. His deposition made Nazism inevitable."** *Announcement inserted in the "In Memoriam" column of* The Times *by The Monarchist League on 5th June, 1974.*

> **"Never have I had warlike ambitions."** *Wilhelm II.*

Right Just another harmless old man feeding the ducks in the park.

88

Principal Characters

AUGUSTA VICTORIA (1858–1921). Wilhelm II's wife, Queen of Prussia and Empress of Germany. Known as "Dona", she was the daughter of Duke Frederick of Schleswig-Holstein-Sonderburg-Augustenburg. She was an amiable woman, by no means good-looking and not very gifted, and apt to bore her husband (whom she married in 1881).

BISMARCK, PRINCE OTTO VON (1815–1898). Appointed Prime Minister of Prussia by Wilhelm I in 1886. In 1871, he became Chancellor of the North German Confederation. The architect of the German Empire, he was known as the Iron Chancellor. He was autocratic, sometimes devious, and often ruthless. He resigned in 1890.

EDWARD VII (1841–1910). King of the United Kingdom from 1901. The relationship between him and his nephew, the Kaiser, was frequently strained, and his determination to make friends with France did little to help matters.

FREDERICK III (1831–88). Wilhelm's father. A retiring individual who was much dominated by his wife. His reign lasted for only six months; when he came to the throne, he was already dying of cancer.

HINZPETER, GEORGE (1827–1907). The son of a school-master in a mining district of Germany, he was Wilhelm's tutor from 1866 to 1879.

SCHLIEFFEN, COUNT ALFRED VON (1833–1913). Served as Chief of Staff to the German Army from 1891 to 1906. Author of the "Schlieffen Plan", which was the basis for German strategy at the outbreak of World War I.

TIRPITZ, GRAND ADMIRAL ALFRED VON (1849–1930). State Secretary for the German Navy from 1897 to 1916. He transformed the fleet from a coastal defence force to a powerful fighting machine.

VICTORIA (1819–1901). Queen of the United Kingdom from 1837, and Wilhelm's grandmother. She was one of the few women whom he regarded with both awe and affection.

VICTORIA (1840–1901). Princess Royal of the United Kingdom and, briefly, German Empress, she was Wilhelm's mother. The eldest child of Queen Victoria, she was a strong and often prejudiced character who made no attempt to accept the German way of life. Her attitude to Wilhelm's disability was so harsh that he believed she disliked him.

WILHELM I (1797–1888). The Kaiser's grandfather, who came to the throne of Prussia in 1861. The Seven Weeks' War with Austria (in 1866) made him extremely popular, and he was proclaimed Emperor of Germany in 1871. He probably had most influence over Wilhelm as a boy.

WILHELM II (1859–1941). King of Prussia and Emperor of Germany from 1888 until his abdication in November, 1918. Behind his arrogant façade, he was self-conscious—even weak. His ambitions for Germany and for himself led to one mistake after another, the greatest of which was to set Europe on fire with World War I. After Germany's defeat, he went into exile in Holland.

Chancellors of Germany during Wilhelm II's reign

BISMARCK, PRINCE OTTO VON, see above.

CAPRIVI, COUNT GEORGE LEO (1831–99). Chancellor 1890–94. Unlike Bismarck, whom he replaced, Caprivi was a mild-mannered man with few ambitions.

HOHENLOHE-SCHILLINGFÜRST, PRINCE CHLODWIC VON (1819–1901). Chancellor 1894–1900. A relative of the Kaiser's wife, he was able to talk with European princes on equal terms and was popular with the people.

BÜLOW, PRINCE BERNHARD VON (1849–1929). Chancellor 1900–1909. He was a fluent speech-maker and experienced diplomat. He had to put right some of the Kaiser's greatest blunders in foreign affairs.

BETHMANN HOLLWEG, THEOBALD VON (1856–1921). Chancellor 1909–1917. He was less assertive than his predecessor, knew little of foreign affairs and was accused of indecisiveness.

MICHAELIS, GEORGE (1857–1936). Chancellor for a few months in 1917. A civil servant by background, he was the only candidate to whom neither the Kaiser nor the German High Command objected.

HERTLING, COUNT GEORGE VON (1843–1919). Chancellor 1917–18. He was an elderly man and almost blind when he came to office. A former professor of philosophy, he admitted that his appointment as Chancellor was "absurd".

BADEN, PRINCE MAX VON (1867–1919). Chancellor in October and November 1918. A prince of the blood royal, he had to contend with riots and mutinies at home and defeat on the Western Front.

Table of Dates

1858   Marriage of Victoria, Princess Royal, to Prince
        Frederick William of Prussia.
        Madness of King Frederick William IV;
        regency of Prince Wilhelm.
1859   Birth of Wilhelm.
1861   Death of Frederick William IV; accession of
        Wilhelm I.
1864   Prussia annexes Schleswig-Holstein.
1866   Prussia overcomes Austria in the "Seven Weeks
        War".
1867   Prince Otto von Bismarck becomes Chancellor
        of Prussia.
1870–1 Franco-Prussian War.
1871   Wilhelm I proclaimed Emperor of Germany at
        Versailles.
1888   Death of Wilhelm I; accession and death of
        Frederick III; Wilhelm II becomes King of
        Prussia and Emperor of Germany.
1889   Strike of German coalminers.
1890   Bismarck resigns.
1894   Alexander III, Tsar of Russia dies; succeeded
        by Wilhelm's cousin, Nicholas II.
1895   Opening of the Kiel Canal.
1896   Jameson Raid in South Africa: Kaiser sends his
        provocative telegram to President Kruger.
1897   Germans help themselves to the Chinese port of
        Tsingtau.
1901   Death of Queen Victoria.
        Death of Wilhelm's mother.
1904   Russia declares war on Japan.
        Germany refused permission to march through
        Belgium.
1905   Kaiser and Tsar of Russia meet off the Finnish
        Island of Björkö and sign treaty.
        The Kaiser lands at Tangier.

Picture Credits

The author and publishers wish to thank the following for their kind permission to reproduce copyright illustrations which appear on the pages mentioned: Mary Evans Picture Library, *frontispiece*, 18, 28, 30, 31, 37, 38, 41, 45, 47, 48, 50, 67, 69 *bottom*, 83; Mansell Collection, 14, 21, 22, 42, 54, 56, 58, 60, 64, 73, 75, 76, 80, 87, 88–89; Radio Times Hulton Picture Library, 12, 17, 24, 25, 33, 52, 55, 79; Imperial War Museum, 61; Farbwerke Hoechst, 39.

Further Reading

Most of the books about this period of German history are written for adults. However, there are two useful Wayland books for secondary schools. Richard Kisch's biography *Bismarck* in the History Makers series (1976) is well-illustrated and for the same reading level as this book. Roger Parkinson's *The Origins of World War One* in the Documentary History series (1970) is a selection of contemporary sources emphasizing the social history of the times.

The following books are suitable for advanced readers or for reference:

Balfour, Michael, *The Kaiser and His Times* (Barrie & Jenkins, 1964; also available from Pelican in paperback). An advanced study of the Kaiser and his influence on the world in general and Germany in particular.

Churchill, Winston S, *Great Contemporaries* (Fontana, 1972). A series of essays on the most significant people of the last hundred years, including the Kaiser.

Taylor, A J P, *The First World War* (Hamish Hamilton, 1963; also available from Penguin in paperback). Although written for adults, this is a lively and readable account of the times, with illustrations.

Wilhelm II, *My Memoirs, 1878–1918* (Cassell, 1922).

Wilhelm II, *My Early Life* (Methuen, 1926). These two autobiographies are now out of print but may be available in public libraries. The style and language level can be judged from the quotations used in this book.

Wilson, Lawrence, *The Incredible Kaiser* (Robert Hale, 1963). A light, humorous book, illustrated with photographs. Now out of print.

Index